Launch Your Business

The 5 Step Solution to Do What You Love, Quit Your Job and Have the Freedom to Travel and Live Life on Your Own Terms

Rosetta Thurman

LIFESTYLE
ENTREPRENEURS
PRESS

Disclaimer and Terms of Use: The Author and Publisher has strived to be as accurate and complete as possible in the creation of this book, notwithstanding the fact that he does not warrant or represent at any time that the contents within are accurate due to the rapidly changing nature of the Internet. While all attempts have been made to verify information provided in this publication, the Author and Publisher assumes no responsibility for errors, omissions, or contrary interpretation of the subject matter herein. Any perceived slights of specific persons, peoples, or organizations are unintentional. In practical advice books, like anything else in life, there are no guarantees of income made. Readers are cautioned to reply on their own judgment about their individual circumstances to act accordingly. This book is not intended for use as a source of legal, medical, health, business, accounting or financial advice. All readers are advised to seek the services of competent professionals in legal, medical, health, business, accounting, and finance fields.

LIFESTYLE ENTREPRENEURS PRESS

Publisher: Jesse Krieger

If you are interested in being published through Lifestyle Entrepreneurs Press, Please email: Jesse@JesseKrieger.com

TABLE OF CONTENTS

INTRODUCTION

Welcome to *Launch Your Business!* I'm Rosetta Thurman, and I'm excited to be with you through the process of getting your business off the ground.

Your business idea may be something you've been thinking about for a long time but have never fleshed out, or you may be relaunching something that you started a while back but never really brought to fruition. You may be starting from scratch, or you may already have a business that's doing all right but not growing as quickly as you'd like. Whether you need to launch, relaunch, or grow your business, you're in the right place! Wherever you fall in any of those categories, I welcome you.

Launching a business is a big decision. It will change your life. I wrote this book because I want to help you become CEO of your life and use your business to craft your ideal life.

A few years ago, I was where you may be now. By all accounts, I had a "good" job. I had a good salary, health insurance, employer contributions to my retirement plan, five weeks of paid time off, money for professional development, flexible hours, the ability to work from home, and even my very own parking spot. I was successful by most measures, but something was missing. I was haunted by a question attributed to Robert H. Schuller:

What would you do if you knew you could not fail?

My answer: work for myself. Write for a living. Travel. Write more.

I had wanted to write a book for a few years, but I could never seem to find the time to do it. Although I liked my job, I couldn't wait to get home each night and work on my own projects. I didn't want to work myself to death and wait until my 60s to finally start living the life I wanted. My life was good, but it wasn't enough. I wanted to it be *great*.

So in 2007, I began blogging about leadership issues in my industry. People started reading my blog and inviting me to speak at events and run workshops. That's how I got my start as a consultant.

In 2008, I announced the opening of Thurman Consulting, even though I was still working a full-time job and had no intentions of leaving anytime soon. I did that to let people know that I was available for speaking and consulting, which became my side hustle—something I did on the side in addition to working my full-time job. By the end of that first year, I had earned $10,000 by speaking and consulting. That was enough for me to see the potential for actually making a living this way.

I kept building my business, and two years later I quit my job to work for myself full-time. In my first year of working for myself, I earned the same amount of money I had been making at my day job. That's when I knew that I could build a successful business doing what I love.

Over time, my business evolved from nonprofit consulting to helping women achieve big goals and beautiful dreams for their lives. My business, Happy Black Woman, reaches thousands of women every month through weekly articles, books, courses, workshops, social events, retreats, and coaching programs. It's been an amazing journey to be able to do what I love and get paid for it! Best of all, it's on my own terms.

That's my goal for you, too. I've written this book to help you make that happen.

I want to commend you for being here. You're embarking on a journey, and this is just the beginning of something that's going to be really amazing for you. Starting a business can be intimidating, but I'll walk you through the steps you'll need to take to start and build a successful business. I'll show you how to take your idea, start earning money from it as quickly as possible, and keep building on it until it's ready to support the life of your dreams. The best time to start is right now, so let's dive in.

I invite you to visit: www.LaunchYourBusinessBook.com for free resources and training to live life on your own terms

To your success,

Rosetta Thurman

Creator of www.HappyBlackWoman.com

CHAPTER 1: GET FOCUSED

In this chapter, we'll talk about how to transform your mindset and make time for your business. These steps will be crucial to making your business a success.

The first thing we'll talk about is the mindset shift that you'll need to make as an entrepreneur. That's really important to your success in your business. We'll also talk about setting an income goal that will help you focus your efforts on the most important revenue-generating activities in your business. Identifying your goal will help you plan out everything you'll need to do to get there.

We'll also cover three powerful strategies to help you remove any negative energy that may be holding you back from achieving success in your business. A successful business isn't just tactics, strategies, and the right to-do list. For many people, the number-one thing holding them back from building a successful business is negative energy. We'll talk about how to deal with that and all the energy-sapping things in our lives that have no business being there.

Finally, we'll talk about how you can create a consistent weekly schedule. This is important. Even if you have a demanding full-time job, kids, and a husband at home, you need to make time for your business. Every entrepreneur needs to create some type of schedule and stick to it. I'll also give you some time-management tips to help you make progress in your business goals every single day.

I know how hard it is to build a business when you have a full-time job and a life full of responsibilities. My business started as a side hustle, and for most people that's the best way to start. That way, you have time to build your business while you still have the security of a full-time job. I'll show you how to find the time and make it work.

All of these pieces come from my own experiences in building my business for two years on the side while I still had a full-time job, as well as the work that I've done with clients over the past few years to help them to build their own businesses. We start with getting focused, because this is one of the biggest challenges to making progress. Once you have that down, everything else flows.

Shifting Your Mindset

The first mindset shift you'll need to make is to begin viewing your endeavor not as a hobby, but as a business. If your business is something you love, chances are it started as a hobby for you. But if you want to build a successful business, you need to treat your business more seriously: as a business, not a hobby.

It starts with realizing that you can have it all—but not all at the same time. There are some choices you'll have to make in support of your business. You're not going to be able to have the same lifestyle that you've had. You're not going to be able to do all the things that you've been doing.

That's not always a bad thing. It just means that you have to tell some people no. In some cases, you've probably been dying to say no anyway. Well, now you have a really good reason: you're building a business. You don't have time to be overextending yourself and saying yes to everybody. You have to make choices about how you spend your time. Some of those choices will be hard, and some will come as a relief as you make more time for what's most important to you.

Some people think of this as a sacrifice, but I don't like to think of it that way. I just think of it as making choices. Some people are not willing to make those choices. They see it as sacrificing time with their friends, and they're not willing to do that. But really, it's a choice to work on their businesses. Ultimately, it's an investment. If you work on your business and keep building it, you can produce some incredible results. If you give up too soon, you'll miss out on all of those things you could have.

As you make your choices, keep the long-term view in mind. Some people get impatient and want to quit their full-time jobs immediately, but that wouldn't have worked for me. I had to build a foundation and a brand, and the more I did that, the more clients I attracted and the more money I made. It's worth taking the time to do it right.

As you work through this book, you'll start to see results. The more you work at it, the more results you'll see. Most business owners start to see a significant return around the three- to five-year mark. At that point, you've been through a launch before, so you know how to put your product or service out there so that people will buy it. You start to build momentum. The money starts coming more easily. Everything starts to flow.

This book will guide you through building the foundation that will see you through those first few years and help you build success. The key is to treat your business like a business, not a hobby. What's the difference? With a hobby, you work on your passion only when you feel inspired. Have you ever tried to write a book that way? It never gets finished, because you don't make time to work on it when you don't feel inspired.

When it's your business, you have to work on it. Taking it seriously means that you sit down at your desk and work on it, even when you don't feel like it. And in that way, you get it done. You end up having something to sell sooner rather than later.

Motivation

To keep yourself going when things get tough, it's important to remember why you're doing this. Why do you want a business? What would it mean for your lifestyle and for your family? It's important to answer that question for yourself so you know what you're working toward.

To get clear on this, I want you to close your eyes for a moment and imagine what it will be like when your business is successful. I want you to fill in the rest of this sentence:

When my business is successful, I will be able to _____.

What's in that blank for you? When your business is successful, what will you be able to do? I want you to write it down and get very clear on your vision of success for your business.

Here are a few answers clients have given me in the past.

- When my business is successful, I'll be able to set my own schedule and structure my days however I want.

- When my business is successful, I'll be able to live wherever I want.

- When my business is successful, I'll have financial freedom.

- When my business is successful, I'll be able to spend more time with my family.

- When my business is successful, I'll be able to travel to places I've always wanted to see.

It's important to get clear on the life you're building with your business so that you can use this vision as your motivation. There will be ups and downs when you're building your business. When you get discouraged, you can look at your vision of what you'll be able to do as a result of your hard work. You can use that vision to build you back up again.

The second thing I want you to think about is how much money you want to earn in your business. Based on that, I want you to set an income goal.

Maybe you would eventually like to be able to replace your income with your business revenue. If that's the case, your salary is the number you would put down here. It might even be a little less if you could live on less. Quitting your job might also reduce some expenses, such as commuting and buying fancy clothes to wear to work.

On the other hand, you may plan to keep your full-time job and just use your business to bring in additional income on the side every year. That would be really great, too.

Either way, it's time to look at some numbers. There's no need to get fancy or get into any difficult math here. Just give your raw, gross numbers.

How much money would you want to earn in your business per year?
_____

Once you have your annual number, I want you to divide that number by 12. That will give you your monthly number.

How much money would you need to bring in per month? _____

From there, divide your monthly number by four to break it down by week.

How much money would you need to bring in per week? _____

Those are your income goals. We begin with numbers, because the main difference between a business and a hobby is that a business makes money. If you're not bringing in money, you have a hobby, not a business. It can also end up being a very expensive hobby, because you're paying for expenses but not bringing in any revenue.

That's why I want you to look at your income goals. There's no right or wrong answer here. I just want you to get thinking about the numbers and write something down, even if it needs to be revised later. By knowing how much money you want to earn in your business, you can start working out what you need to charge for your products and services. We'll work on that in Chapter Two, but first you need to be focused and productive. That's the foundation that will support you in doing all the marketing and establishing clarity around your products and services.

What Holds You Back

For many people, what holds us back is not being focused and not being productive. I've made a list of some common mindset obstacles that keep us from being productive:

- Procrastination

- Perfectionism

- Distractions

- Self-sabotage

- Fear of failure

- Fear of success

- Lack of confidence

For many people, the fear of success may sound counterintuitive, but it's something that a lot of women struggle with. Many of us worry about this: when I become successful, or as I continue becoming more successful, am I going to lose friends? Are people going to look at me differently? Who am I going to hang out with? What if my family starts asking me for money all the time?

These are real concerns, so we have to be aware. As you go through the process of launching your business, be on the lookout for these patterns and behaviors. There's no need to identify with them too much. (We all procrastinate sometimes, but that doesn't mean we need to see ourselves as procrastinators.) Just notice these obstacles when they pop up, accept that this is normal, and work around them.

How to Clear Away Negative Energy

I want to give you three ways that can help you clear away any negative energy that might be keeping you from moving forward in your business. I believe very firmly in the power of energy and what you are attracting into your life, and I want to help you set up a positive atmosphere for business success.

Clearing the Clutter

The first way to clear out old negative energy is clearing the clutter. Holding on to clutter from the past could be holding you back from receiving success in your business. If you have a lot of clutter in your life, it will be hard for you to move forward. You may have noticed that it can be hard to concentrate when your house feels dirty or messy. A messy house can also make it difficult to get out the door, because you can't find anything.

Clutter holds you back, so you want to clear it out—especially in the space where you're going to be working on your business. If your workspace is always covered with papers or other things, it would definitely be worth it for you to take some time and get that space in order. Get rid of everything that you're not using. If you haven't done that yet, take the time to do it this week.

The reason why we clear clutter is to make space for new things. That's as simple as it gets: you want to clear out the old to make room for the new. For our purposes, the new is success in your business, so clear out all the old to make room for the new.

Remove Negative People from Your Life

The second way to clear out negative energy is to remove negative people from your life. These are the people who lower your energy whenever you're around them.

This is not to say that people are bad. It just means that you have to manage your energy. When you're building a business, you need high energy, or at least moderate energy. There's a lot to do, and it's hard to get things done when you're low on energy. To be productive, you want to cultivate a high-energy state and a positive mindset. People who deplete your energy make that harder, so you may need to stop hanging around those people. (You probably already know who they are.)

I'm not saying you need to call people and tell them you're removing them from your life. Just make a mental list of all the people in your life who bring you down. Commit to spending as little time around those people as possible, especially as you work to launch your business.

Stop Doing Unproductive Activities

Finally, to maximize your energy, I want you to refrain from participating in unproductive activities. For many people, this is a big challenge. One specific thing I'm going to recommend is that you don't watch any television for the next six weeks as you build the foundation for your business. This may sound extreme to you, but it's really important.

Again, we're managing our energy, and TV is full of negative energy: arguments, sensational news, gossip, and people judging each other. I especially limit my exposure to the news. You know what they say: "If it bleeds, it leads." All that negative news depletes your energy. It makes you worry about what the world is coming to, and it may even make you question the possibility of your own success. I want to caution you to manage that and refrain from doing things that are unproductive.

Another big unproductive activity is mindless surfing on the internet. This is huge for many people: when you feel frustrated or want to procrastinate, you might go to Facebook or Instagram and start scrolling through photos. You really have to catch yourself when you're doing that and refrain from it. While you're getting your business off the ground, you need to focus. During this time, the goal is to create more than you consume.

To launch your business, you're going to be creating a lot of things. You're going to be creating ideas. You're going to be creating products and services. You're going to be creating your brand and your marketing materials. To do these things, you need your brain, and you need it to be operating at high levels. That's why it's important to manage your energy.

What we're working on is transforming your mindset for success. It doesn't happen overnight, but you can make it easier for yourself by clearing the clutter and eliminating negative people and unproductive activities.

Here's one of my favorite quotes:

> "Good things happen to those who hustle."
>
> —Chuck Noll, Head Coach of Pittsburgh Steelers from 1969 to 1991

This truly embodies the spirit of the entrepreneur. When you work, you get results, so I want to make sure that nothing is hindering you from doing that. Television and mindless surfing are the two most obvious unproductive activities, but we all have more. I want you to make a list of things to stop doing. Instead of a "To-Do List," it's a "Stop Doing List."

As you're thinking about this, I want you to answer this question:

What did the old you do that the new you just doesn't have time for anymore?

The old you wasn't building her business, or wasn't growing it, or wasn't launching anything. But now that you've taken the step to read this book and invest in yourself, some changes have to happen. I want you to ask yourself this: who do you have to be in order to achieve that income goal that you wrote down? Again, a lot of it comes down to managing your energy and choosing the best use of your time. The old you probably did a lot of things that the new you just doesn't have time for anymore.

To give you an example, I'll share something that was on my "Stop Doing List" as I built my business over the years. I had a friend who always had man problems. She always had a boyfriend who wasn't treating her right, and she would call me late at night crying all the time. Maybe I needed to get to bed and sleep because I had a big speaking engagement in the morning, or maybe I was still working on something, but there she was, calling me in tears. This kept going on and on until I had to have a talk with her and say, "You know, the old me would've stayed up with you all night all the time, but I can't live my life like that anymore."

We both realized that she was always calling me for help, but what was I really getting out of the relationship? The new me didn't have time for that anymore. I didn't have time to be a free counselor, and I learned that friendship needs to be a two-way street.

We all have things that we need to stop doing so that we can be successful, and you're going to make your own list of things that you need to stop doing.

Start Accepting Support

Just as we all have things we need to stop doing, there are also some things we need to start doing. One big thing you may have to start doing is to ask your family and friends for help. The people around you who are supportive will want to help you—so let them!

For many of us, that's not easy. Often, even if someone offers to help or asks if there's anything he/she can do, our default response is, "Oh, no, don't worry yourself. I don't want to impose upon you." But you can't do everything yourself. As you're building your business, you're going to have to learn how to accept help.

In addition to accepting an extra hand from your friends or family, you may also want to start outsourcing some household or administrative tasks. For example, you may get someone else to do the cleaning. That's one of the first things that I outsourced. Even before I quit my job, when I started getting out there with my speaking, I hired a cleaning service. I was working full-time, doing my blog in the morning and in the evening, traveling, and using my vacation time to do some speaking engagements. Meanwhile, I was also in a relationship. My boyfriend used to joke that the only time he saw me was at home, so I didn't want to spend my time at home cleaning. I wanted to spend that time with my partner, so I hired a cleaning service. Surprisingly, in most cities, you can get some really good deals on cleaning every two weeks, once a month, or even once a week. You may want to look into that so you can free up some of your time.

Another time-saver is having a grocery service deliver your groceries. I know that personally, I spend a lot of time in the grocery store. You have to drive there, get all the food, and drive back, not to mention preparing the food when you get home. Getting someone else to do tasks like that can free up some of your time.

As your business grows, you'll want to think about administrative and technical support. When we talk about getting online and doing your social media, you don't have to do all of those things yourself. You could think about hiring an intern or a virtual assistant. I've had several interns and virtual assistants over the years. Again, when you look around, you can get good people for not much money.

These are a few simple strategies to help you be productive and stay productive. It doesn't need to be complicated. These are things that you can incorporate into your lifestyle easily.

Setting a Schedule

Once you have your mindset and energy in order, think about productivity. One key to productivity is working on your business when you're at your best. So, I put the question to you:

When are you at your most focused and productive?

I want you to notice and observe when you're at your best. For some people, it's first thing in the morning; for others, it's late at night. Whenever it is for you, you want to use the best of your time on your business. It just makes sense: when you're at your most creative, you're far more likely to write a great sales page or flyer or brochure, and it will be easier for you to do. So you need to figure out when that prime time is for you and make the most of it.

Once you're clear on that, you can make a work schedule for yourself. As you work on building your business, I suggest that you carve out at least 20 hours a week to work on your business, and make that your weekly schedule. When I did this, it revolutionized my business.

By making a schedule, you're committing to actually using that time for your business. If you're working full-time, it's important to make sure you carve out enough time for your business and all of your other commitments. And if you're not working full-time, it may be even more important. The strange thing about having a wide-open schedule is that it seems like there's infinite time to do everything, so it's easy to put things off and get very little done. Either way, by making a schedule for yourself and sticking with it, you make sure that the important things get done.

One way to find 20 hours in a week is to find 10 hours during the week and 10 hours on the weekend. If you're a morning person, obviously that's going to be the time when you want to use your brainpower for your business, so you may get up early and carve out two hours each day before you go to work. If you're an evening person, then you'll want to use the hours after work. If you're not watching TV anymore, that will free up some time for working on your business. Another option is to do one hour before work and one hour after, or to use a lunch break for one hour each day.

For some people, working in the evening is harder than it sounds because it means they have to start leaving work on time. If you struggle with this, remember: What did the old you do that the new you just doesn't have time for anymore? One answer might be working late. Maybe the old you was working late just because you like to be helpful, and you want people to like you, and you really want the team to succeed. If that's you, you'll have to start setting some boundaries.

Whichever way you decide to do it, you want to find two hours a day during the week for your business. That gives you 10 hours during the week.

Some people can't work on the business every day, and that's fine, too. For example, if you're busy on Wednesdays, maybe you'll work four hours on Fridays and two hours a day on Monday, Tuesday, and Thursday.

Once you've found 10 hours during the week, you can find another 10 hours on the weekends to get your 20 hours a week. You may want to split that up as five hours on Saturday and five hours on Sunday, or you may do all 10 hours on one day so you can have one day completely off. It's up to you, and this doesn't mean you can't sleep in on Saturday mornings anymore or you can't go to church on Sunday. You can do those things; just work on the business later in the day. For instance, if you like to sleep late on Saturday, you might sleep until noon and then work on the business from 1:00 to 6:00.

Again, as you're thinking about what schedule will work for you, keep in mind the times of the day and week when you're at your most focused and productive.

Now, creating your schedule is just the first step. Once you've done that, I want you to go into your calendar and block off that time. Whether you use a paper calendar or a digital calendar like Google Calendar, go into your calendar and actually block off that time for your business.

When I first started doing this, I'd just write "Work on my business" for each of these blocks of time. Now I'm more specific on what I'm supposed to be doing during that time, but in the beginning it's fine to just say, "Work on business," "work on business," "work on business."

Whether you're working an outside job or not, it's important to do this. You want to make the schedule and block out that time to make sure it gets done. You can live a good life, work very hard on your business, and still have time to spend with your family and friends and do other things you enjoy. It starts with creating a schedule and sticking to that schedule. When you have people in your life, it helps to let them know that you have a schedule. That way, they know when you're available and when you're not, so it's easier for them to take your work on your business seriously.

Making a schedule is all about respecting your own time. The worst thing is wasted time. You can always get money back, but you can't get time back. Once years are gone, they're gone. That's why I'm so excited and proud of you for taking this step to launch your business, because this commitment could lead to years of business growth for you.

Making a schedule helps you respect your own time and really make the most of it. Although it may seem very basic, it can be transformative for your business because it gets you in the habit of working on your business regularly and getting things done all the time. Those efforts start to add up quickly.

Homework

1. Determine your income goals for your business.

    a. How much money do you want to make each year?

    b. Divide that by 12 to get how much money you need to make each month.

    c. Divide your monthly number by 4 to get how much money you need to make each week.

2. Use a blank calendar to help you create your weekly schedule. Mark off the hours you use for sleep, work, and other obligations. Then mark 20 hours a week to work on your business. (One way to do this is two hours per weekday and 10 hours on the weekend.) Finally, block off those hours in your calendar, whether you use a paper calendar or an electronic one.

3. Make your "Stop Doing" list. What did the old you do that the new you—the you who is going to build a successful business—doesn't have time for anymore?

CHAPTER 2: GET CLARITY. FIND YOUR SWEET SPOT AND IDENTIFY YOUR IDEAL CLIENTS

At this point, you may not have a clear idea of what you want to do in your business or what your sweet spot is. This chapter will help you cut through a lot of confusion. If you're not sure what your business is about, what you should be doing, or whom you should be doing it for, read on! If you already have a good idea of what you're going to be doing with your business, this chapter will help you refine that.

This chapter is all about getting clarity. I'm going to take you through a process that will help you find your sweet spot and identify your ideal client. As we mentioned before, you need to know who is most likely to buy your services. Sometimes that person is different than you may think, so prepare to be surprised.

Up until now, you may have felt scattered in your business, like you're juggling too many ideas and you're not sure what to focus on. We're going to eliminate that feeling by finding your business sweet spot.

We're going to start by helping you define your brand to attract the perfect prospects to your doorstep. Then, we're going to go through a step-by-step process for identifying your ideal clients and customers. This will help you figure out where these people are, how to find them, and how to attract them to your business.

We're also going to work on finding the perfect words to explain what you do. This skill will keep you from being tongue-tied and flustered at networking events. Many people shy away from networking opportunities because they don't know what to say. By the end of this chapter, that will not be you!

Finding Your Business Sweet Spot

To start to identify your business sweet spot, I'm going to give you a little test that I came up with. I was thinking about what it feels like when you're building a business, and you do so many things and have so many ideas that you feel scattered. The problem is that when you feel scattered, everyone else also feels scattered and unsure of whether they should hire you. I like to compare it to a Chinese restaurant.

Now, I have nothing against Chinese restaurants or Chinese food. I love Chinese food, but I am a foodie in general. Whatever I eat, I want it to be really good.

In Baltimore, where I live, there are all these little Chinese restaurants. The problem is very few of them actually specialize in Chinese food. They have Chinese food on one side, but then they'll also serve pizza or soul food. You'll see one place serving fried chicken, collard greens, pepperoni pizza, and chow mein. I saw one restaurant serving Chinese, Japanese, and Korean all on the same menu.

When I see things like this, I always think, "Doesn't this place have good Chinese food? If so, why do they have all these other things? And why would I think that this Chinese restaurant should be good at making pizza? Are you a Chinese restaurant, or are you not? What are you doing?"

Most people want something good when they go out to eat. Personally, I would prefer to go to a Chinese restaurant that's known for the best chow mein, the best orange chicken, or the best egg foo yung, rather than a restaurant that has all sorts of things. When these restaurants try to make everything, usually none of it is very good. It's only by specializing that you can make something great. That's true in food, and it's true in business. That's what I call the Chinese Restaurant Test.

If you look at your business and it looks like a Chinese restaurant in Baltimore with nine different cuisines, it's very hard for people to tell what you're good at. That's why it's actually best to be known for one thing and do it well, rather than trying to do everything.

I know this is a big challenge when you're creative. You probably have many talents and great ideas—but that doesn't mean you can do all of those things well. Trying to do many different things also makes it hard to market yourself in a cohesive way, so that potential customers know what you're about. It's better to be known for one thing than to have people confused because you have too many cuisines in your restaurant. Focusing on one specialty isn't only better for your business, it's better for you, too. It will help you stop feeling so scattered.

To do that, we're going to narrow things down and get clear on your business sweet spot. The best way to find your sweet spot is to look where your passion, your expertise, and the marketplace intersect.

You've probably heard part of this before. Many people say you should build your business around doing something you love. That's true, but it's not enough. It also needs to be something you're good at and something that there's a market for. If you have a very specific passion with a very specific expertise and only two other people in the world are interested in it, then you're going to have a hard time finding a clientele. That's not your business sweet spot.

To help you find your sweet spot, we're going to start by looking a little closer at each of these three criteria.

Finding Your Gift

For the passion part of the equation, think about what you love to do. Really, that's the whole point of this book: to figure out how to get paid to do what you love. This is really important. I would never recommend that anybody start a business just because it's a good business idea. You have to enjoy it. In business, there are highs and lows, and the lows can get really low. You need to love what you do so you can make it through those lows.

I can tell you this because I've been there. In fact, almost every business owner has at least one story like this. In 2011, I lost a huge client. As a result, my revenue went down. I wasn't making as much money as I needed to make, and in my mind, that meant I had failed. I got very depressed. Thankfully, I was able to take my own coaching advice, do what I needed to do, and bounce back. I'm not sure I could have done that if I wasn't passionate about my business. I wouldn't have had the same level of motivation.

In business, there are always going to be difficult times. You have to do something you love so that you can push through those difficult times. You'll make it if you love what you do, because if you love it enough, you'll fight for it.

So, what do you love to do? What do you love doing so much that you would do it for free?

As you read this book, this may be an easy question to answer because you're already doing it for free. If so, take heart, because you're not going to be doing it for free for long. That's why you're reading this book.

Another way to ask this is "Where is your heart?" You know your heart. Think about where your heart is and write an answer.

As you think about these questions, something may come out that hasn't come out before, or you may start to see things in a different way.

Identifying Your Expertise

For your expertise, think about what areas you have experience in. You don't have to have a Ph.D. to be an expert. Just think about what you're good at. What is your gift?

That's a beautiful question to ask yourself, because you already know the answer. It's been with you for years—something you've always had, like a gift for helping other people, a gift for communicating, a gift for inspiring people, a gift for making things clear, a gift for writing, a gift for problem solving, or a gift at helping other people relieve stress. It's something you've always done in some form or fashion.

For me, I know that my gift is teaching. Ever since I was little, I've known that I would teach in some way. In my case, it wasn't elementary school or high school, but college. I taught undergrad and graduate courses, and now I teach online courses. Also, when I'm speaking, I'm teaching.

As you think about these questions, I want you to not only get clear on your expertise, but also to validate it. It doesn't matter what qualifications you have or whether anyone else validates your expertise. All that matters is that it's valid to you. Otherwise, it will hold you back from making money. (We'll cover that more in Chapter Three.)

A lot of people discount their own expertise, but if you have ten years of experience in something, that makes you an expert. Even if you have two or three years of experience in something, that makes you an expert to the person who's brand new to it, so don't hold back from this question. Expertise can mean a lot of things, and it can look like a lot of things. Make sure you give yourself credit for yours.

Finding a Marketplace

The third aspect of your business sweet spot is your marketplace. It's important to ask yourself whether there's a market for your product or service. I often work with women who want to build a business around something they're passionate about and good at, but they don't know what their market would be or even whether there is a market for what they want to do.

To begin identifying your marketplace, ask yourself these questions:

- What kind of people would be highly interested in what you do? Who would be highly interested in your area of passion and expertise?

- Who needs what you have to offer?

- Who can you help?

For many people, the most important question is "Who can you help?" It's important to look at this very closely, because sometimes the people you want to help may not want to be helped. For example, I've had clients who really had a passion for helping youth and showing them how to make better choices. But unless the youth are interested in what they do, want the service enough to pay for it, and have the means to do so, they're not a viable marketplace for this service.

Many people may be interested in what you do and think it's cool, but that doesn't mean that they're so interested that they would give you money. That's the distinction we need to make here. You need to find someone who has the interest and the means to pay you.

Going back to our example, youth might need what you have to offer, but that doesn't mean that they're highly interested in it. If you want to work with youth, you may need to shift your focus from the youth to the parents or school administrators. They need you *and* they're highly interested in what you do, because it's going to help the youth. They're the ones who will pay you, not the youth, so they're your marketplace. It's important to make that distinction.

Now that we've been through each aspect, think again about the big picture.

- Where is your heart?

- What is your niche?

- Who can you help?

This is another way of saying that your passion, your expertise, and your marketplace have to intersect.

Many people have only two of the three elements. Maybe you have a passion and you see a marketplace for it, but you're not good at it. If that's the case, is it something you can develop? What would it take to become good at it?

For other people, they have the passion and they're good at it, but they can't see a marketplace yet. If this is you, hang in there. We're going to look at your ideal client later in the chapter, and that may help you get clear on your marketplace.

Finally, you may have expertise and a marketplace, but you're not passionate about it. In my opinion, that's the worst kind of business to have. You could be really good at something, find a market for it, and do it for a while to bring in money, but if your passion isn't there, it's very likely that you'll burn out. When it comes time to do the work, you'd rather be on Facebook because your heart isn't in it.

You really want to have all three things aligned. And let's be real: when those things align, it doesn't make it that much easier, but at least you're on the right track. Some people end up starting businesses where they know they could be good at something and they know there's a market out there, because they think it's going to be easier. And really, it's not. It's all hard, so you might as well choose something you're passionate about. That way, at least you'll be making as strong a start as possible.

As you're working on this, if you still have questions, there's another assessment I can recommend: the VIA Survey of Character Strengths. This assessment was developed by Dr. Martin Seligman, one of the founders of the positive psychology movement. It helps you discover your top five signature strengths. I first did this assessment in 2006-2007 when I was making shifts in my career, and it really helped me get clear on my strengths.

To take the assessment, go to authentichappiness.org. You have to register on the site to take the assessment, but there's no cost involved. Give yourself at least 40 minutes to take it. It's about 240 questions and well worth the time.

Once you've taken the assessment, you'll know your five signature strengths. Then you can use them in your business by building your brand around them and offering products and services that build on them.

To give you an idea what I mean, I'll share my five signature strengths.

- **Ingenuity/originality.** This is all about thinking of new and productive ways to conceptualize and do things. For me, that plays a part in my writing, blogging, and authorship (including books, classes, and courses). It also helps as a strength in many other aspects of life and business. If you're someone who has creativity as a strength, you'll be frustrated if you choose a career or a business where you can't use that strength. That's why I made sure to incorporate this into my business.

- **Curiosity.** This means exploring, discovering, and taking an interest in ongoing experiences for their own sake. For me, this plays a part in my coaching, consulting, and blogging. Being curious helps me ask powerful questions when I'm coaching—it's easy to ask questions when you're curious. Instead of telling people what to do, I'll ask, "Why is this going on?" or "What would happen if you did this differently?" That helps them find their own answers. Because curiosity is one of my signature strengths, this comes naturally—I don't have to work at it.

- **Perspective/wisdom.** With this strength, I can provide wise counsel to others and help them make sense of the world. I can step back and help people see the bigger picture. This is another strength that I use all the time in my coaching and consulting. Although most of my coaching clients and students are older than I am, they often say that I have an old soul or I'm wise for my age. I take that as a compliment.

- **Hope**. This strength encompasses optimism and future-mindedness, expecting the best in the future and working to achieve it. I use this strength in my coaching, speaking, and training. In coaching, it allows me to offer an optimistic reading of the future to help my clients get through the hard times. When they get discouraged, I can lift them back up. In speaking, this strength is the source of the motivation and inspiration in my talks. It also helps when I'm training people. A lot of people don't like taking training, but I help them see what they're working toward and teach them to focus on that.

- **Social intelligence.** This strength means being aware of the motives and feelings of other people and yourself. This also helps me a lot in coaching, speaking, training, and group dynamics.

Looking at my strengths, it's obvious where I shine, and I've built my services around that. In fact, that's all I do in my business. If you do what you're best at, it's easy to shine, and that's how you get repeat business. That's what I recommend.

So, if you're not sure what you should be doing, this assessment may help you get some clarity. It may affirm something that you've been on the fence about. For instance, if you're not sure whether you should be a coach, looking at your signature strengths may make it obvious that it's something you'd be great at. Knowing that will help you have confidence as you start offering that service.

Branding

Once you know your strengths, you can use them to build your brand. To define your brand, I want you to ask yourself which three words you want people to think of when they think of you. Really, your brand is what people say about you when you're not in the room. So, how would someone describe you, and how do you *want* people to describe you?

For my business, I've built my brand around being informational, inspirational, and motivational. Those are the three words that I want people to think of when they think of me, so I deliberately present myself that way. For example, to show that I'm informational, I publish a lot of articles on my blog for free. That shows that I have good information on a variety of topics related to personal development and entrepreneurship.

Being informational is part of my brand, but it's not enough. A lot of people give information, so I also put myself out there as someone who is inspirational. I show people what's possible. This is important because many people ask me how to convince people that they need your product or service. In reality, you don't need to convince them of anything. What you need to do is show them what's possible, and that can be very inspiring. To understand what I mean, think about car commercials.

Regardless of the brand, they don't tell you "We just came out with a new car. You really need this car, and we're going to tell you why." What they do is show you and try to inspire you with the image of what your life could be like if you bought that Lexus or Mercedes. Or if it's an SUV, they show you that all your kids can fit in there. They show you camping trips and images of the family doing things together. After seeing that commercial, you might be inspired and think: Wow, I do want to have more time with my family. Maybe this SUV could help me do that.

You don't need to be convinced that you want more time with your kids all together in one car and doing great things together. The commercial simply taps into that desire and shows you that this product could help you achieve that goal.

Basically, commercials tap into existing goals and show people that, if they had the product, it could help them achieve their goals more quickly, more easily, more effectively, or less expensively. Even for things like hair and body products, it's not all about the product but what you would be like if you had it. Think about that as you work on your brand. What goals do people have that you can help them fulfill? How can you inspire people and show them what's possible?

In my brand, I don't just inform and inspire—I also motivate. Again, there are many people who inspire and many people who have good information, but I want to help my clients by motivating them to take action. So I'm always talking about achieving your goals, taking baby steps, trying tools, implementing strategies. I don't just want to inspire people; I want to motivate them to use that inspiration to take action.

Those are the three words in my brand: informational, inspirational, and motivational. For your brand, I want you to think about what three words you want people to think about when they think of you.

This three-word brand will come into play in all of your marketing materials, from your website to your business cards. It can also help you when you talk about yourself in networking settings. Instead of stammering and trying to think of how to answer, you can use your three-word brand as a starting point for talking about what you do.

Ideal Client

Next, we're going to talk about your ideal client. This ties into your three-word brand because the ideal client should think of those three words when he or she thinks of you. So, who is your ideal client or customer? I have four questions to help you visualize this person. I'm going to use "she" here, but of course your ideal client could also be male.

Question 1: Who is she?

Another way to look at this is "What does she want?" It's important to note that your ideal client has to want something. If she doesn't want anything, she's not going to buy anything. You can't make people want something they don't want. You have to tap into something they already want, and offer a solution to help them.

For example, one possible ideal client could be a young professional who wants to advance in her career. This is an important distinction: there may be many young professionals who do not want to advance in their careers. They are not your ideal clients. It's not enough to just say "young professional," because not all young professionals want help. There's a certain segment of young professionals who are more ambitious, who are more interested in self-improvement and career advancement. If they believe you can help them achieve this goal, they're likely to be interested in your help.

Remember, your goal is not to find people who you think need your help, beat them upside the head, and get mad when they don't buy from you. Instead, you want to find the people who want something that you can help them get.

Question 2: What does she struggle with?

Another way to ask this is "What problems does she want to solve?" For the example of the young professional who wants to advance in her career, maybe she doesn't feel confident enough to ask for a raise or a promotion, or to position herself for a leadership opportunity. Maybe she wants to apply for a new job, but she doesn't feel that she has enough experience. Those might be problems that she wants to solve.

Question 3: Why does she need me?

How can you help her solve her problem? This is important because if there's no perception that you can help her, then she's not going to buy from you. Continuing in our example, maybe you can help her solve her problem by helping her increase her confidence and giving her a roadmap to a new job in six months. That's a clear way in which you could help her solve her problems and achieve something she wants.

Question 4: Where does she hang out?

As you look at who your ideal client is, it's important to think about where you can find her. What websites does she visit? What magazines does she read? What kinds of groups or associations would she belong to?

For example, she might belong to Ambitious Young Professionals of Pittsburgh. Look for groups in your area, or even national groups. That's a great way to really hone in on the people who want to advance in their careers, because only motivated people will spend the time and money to join these groups. Those are the people who will be interested enough to pay you. You want to find out where those people are and meet them there with your marketing, whether it's an ad, getting an article published on a website, or speaking at an event.

These four questions are juicy. They really produce great answers. To give you an example, I'll show you my ideal client for my business, Happy Black Woman.

She longs to build a business doing what she loves, but she doesn't know where to start and finds all the information out there overwhelming. She's ready to beat procrastination and begin taking action. She longs to connect with like-minded women. She wants to find a community where she's fully supported and not judged.

In particular, I want you to notice the last sentence. This is something that I know my ideal client wants. As a result, I started doing more live events to connect with people in person. My ideal client does not necessarily have friends and family who understand and support her in the way that like-minded women can. Even if she does have supportive friends and family, she may want more support from a group that's focused on business, so I tailored my products and services to meet that need.

I keep my ideal client in mind for everything I do in my business. I use language that would attract her. I write blog posts on topics that will interest her. Whenever I write, my ideal client is the person I'm writing to. When I create programs, she's the person I'm creating my programs for.

As you think about your ideal client in your business, think about your past clients if you've had any. Who were they? What did they need from you? Where did you find them? Of course, if you didn't like your clients, then you don't want to think about them—it's better to start from scratch. But if you've had good experiences, that may give you some clues.

How to Say What You Do

Once you've thought about your sweet spot, your branding, and your ideal client, you can use that to help you talk about what you do. Many people struggle with an "elevator pitch" or explaining what they do clearly in just a sentence or two. But it's actually pretty easy. Here's a template that you can use.

I provide _____ for _____ so they can _____.

The first blank is your sweet spot. The second is your ideal client, and the third is the transformation you offer. So basically you're saying how you help people, who you help, and what exactly you do.

I have a great example that I hope will inspire you. This is from Chemise Cameron, who came to one of our Happy Black Woman happy hours in Charlotte, North Carolina, a few years ago. I've followed her journey to become a respected Web designer, and she is very clear about what she does. Here's her statement:

I create simple and pretty blog designs for style and beauty bloggers who are ready to step up their game and get more sponsorship opportunities.

Her sweet spot is creating simple, pretty blog designs, and her ideal client is style and beauty bloggers who are ready to step up their game. (Of course, there are some style and beauty bloggers who are not ready to step up their game. They're not her ideal clients.) The transformation that she offers is to help them get more sponsorship opportunities. By stating it in this form, it's very simple and clear.

Here's another example. This is my "What I Do" statement.

I provide training and coaching for women who are ready to take action on their goals so that they can create their ideal lives and businesses.

Again, notice my ideal client. You don't want to be offering services for people who don't need or want them. That's why I didn't just say, "I provide training and coaching for women." Not all women want or need training or coaching, but women who are ready to take action on their goals are often looking for some type of guidance. Otherwise they would have done it already and they wouldn't need me.

Finally, "so that they can create their ideal lives and businesses" explains the transformation that I offer. That's the big picture: I want you to have the life you want, and I know you need to take action in order to do that. I can help support you. I have tools, I have worksheets, I have coaching, and we can talk on the phone. I can provide a neutral support system and hold you accountable so you can create your ideal life and business.

Some people struggle with identifying the transformations they offer. Another way to think of this is to consider the end reason why people would want to buy your product. For example, if you sell jewelry, why would someone buy your jewelry? For many women, they buy beautiful, handcrafted jewelry so that they can express their creativity. They express themselves through what they wear, whether it's earrings or shoes or a pretty scarf. You don't have to offer a service in order to offer a transformation—this template can fit any type of business.

As you work on your "What I Do" statement, remember that it doesn't have to be perfect. You can keep refining it as you go. But writing it down now will help you gain clarity and put together all of the pieces we've covered in this chapter.

Homework

1. Find your business sweet spot.

   a. What do you love doing?

    b.   What are you good at?

    c.   Where is the market?

    d.   What's the intersection of those three areas?

2. Determine your three-word brand. There's no need to overthink this. Just pick three words that you want people to think of when they think of you. As you move forward, these three words will shape your business communications—how you talk about yourself, the kind of blog posts you write, the articles you write to market yourself—because you want to be doing things that cause people to think about those words in relation to you.

3. Identify your ideal client.

    a.   Who is she?

    b.   What does she struggle with?

    c.   Why does she need you?

    d.   Where does she hang out?

4. Create your "What I Do" statement. Once you've done the first three pieces, this becomes much easier.

CHAPTER 3: GET PAID

This chapter is about how to develop products and services that people will pay you for. You'll learn how to choose which products and services to focus on to get the most return for the time and energy you invest. My new Multiple Income Streams Model is also included in this chapter, which will show you 10 practical ways to monetize and give structure to your passion.

This chapter also includes a special pricing template, which will give you a sense of how much to charge for your products and services and ensure that you get paid what you're worth. This is based on my experience in different industries, as well as that of my clients. I'll also guide you through the process of creating sales pages.

You'll learn about all the tools you need to start earning money through your business, and you'll have a checklist that shows you exactly what you might be missing. These guides can really help you to move your business forward or give you the necessary steps to prepare your business for launch.

You can see we have a lot to cover, but let's begin with a little inspiration. I want to congratulate you on what you have already accomplished. You've made the decision to start, launch, or grow your business. You've made an investment in reading this book, and you've come this far. You haven't allowed fear of the unknown or anything else to deter you from starting your business, so congratulations.

Making Money

The core theme of this chapter is making money. In Chapter Two, you did the work of figuring out your sweet spot, coming up with your ideal client profile, and creating your "What I Do" statement. Now you need to know how to turn your business into one that makes money. You know what you do and who you want to serve; now it's time to create a structure.

But first, I'd like to offer a few cautionary suggestions. As we discuss charging for your services, some limiting beliefs may come up for you. I want to identify them so that you can be aware of them and not allow them to interfere with your success. Talking about pricing or charging for services makes some people feel uncomfortable. Women especially tend to feel that, if they are doing what they love, it's not OK to charge for it or charge a decent fee for it. There are many other people doing what you're doing, and they're making a good income doing it. We may know this, but when it comes to ourselves, we may still not feel that we deserve fair payment.

There are many potential limiting beliefs that may come up for you in the process of setting up your business. If you notice them, make a note of them.

Some of these limiting beliefs come from our upbringing or what our parents said about money. You may have grown up with your family saying that money doesn't grow on trees, or that money is hard to come by. If you grew up like I did, then you probably understand. When I was a kid, we didn't have a lot of money. We lived in the projects. We learned to be happy that we had a roof over our heads and food in the refrigerator.

When we're raised with these beliefs, they can keep us from being aware of our own worth and what's possible for us. In short, many of our beliefs about money are driven by a feeling of scarcity.

As you build your business, it's crucial that you let go of these beliefs and really be conscious of how you think and speak about money. We want to attract money to us, and if we're thinking or saying that money is hard to come by, then it can be difficult to charge a reasonable price for our products and services. Based on your life experiences, you may think everybody in the world is having a hard time with money, but that's not true. The client across from you may have a pocketful ready to spend. You really have to be aware of these limiting beliefs.

For your business to work, it's absolutely essential that you accept that you deserve to earn money. If you give your products and services away for free, then you can't make money in your business, and you may never be able to earn a living doing what you love to do. So you really have to shift your thinking from "I already do this for free, so why should I get paid for it?" to "My gifts are valuable."

I had to change this mindset for myself, too. At first, I didn't realize there was any value in what I was providing. When I realized that the organizations I was speaking for were charging an entry fee for people to come and hear me speak, that value became clear to me. The event hosts had already assigned a value to what I do. If I didn't charge for that value, it was my own loss.

Another mindset shift you'll need to make is to start viewing your services from a customer's perspective rather than your own. You may think, "I would never pay that much for XYZ." After completing the ideal client exercise, it should be clear to you that you are not your ideal client. Your ideal client wants what you can provide. Just because you would never pay $2,000 for a coach doesn't mean that your ideal client feels the same. People who need what you offer will pay to get that value. As you look at different offerings in your industry, work on shifting your thinking from "I would never pay that much for that" to "Why would someone else pay that much for this?" to "This person's work deserves my investment."

Also, be aware of how you talk about money and investment in your own life. Sometimes in the coaching industry, I hear people talk about the cost to hear a guru or renowned coach speak: "It costs $3,000? Who does she think she is to charge $3,000 for an event?" Well, there's value in what that speaker does, and there are people who see that value and pay for it.

Be careful how you speak about the products and services of others. My mentor calls it business karma: if you attack someone else's work or pricing, you may find that no one is registering for your event or buying your products and services. You may feel uncomfortable charging a higher price, because you just talked about the next person who was charging a high price.

We really don't want to limit ourselves by attacking others. When you feel these kinds of thoughts coming up for you, take a moment to notice them. Then keep moving with the structure we're providing here.

Now that we've covered limiting beliefs that could hold you back, we're going to talk about how to earn revenue. To do that, we have to create products and services that people want and are willing to buy.

Your Signature Product or Service

To be profitable, you have to achieve clarity on which products and services to offer in your business. To avoid becoming overwhelmed, it's best to focus on one core product or service to begin with. This is what I call your signature product or service. It's what your ideal clients most need and want to buy from you, so it really has to do with the core of your sweet spot. Your signature product or service must be in line with the sweet spot you've identified, since that's where you're going to make the most money.

My sweet spot is writing books that inspire, move, or entertain. If I came up with a different product or service because I was afraid to put out a book, I wouldn't be capitalizing on my strengths. Don't make this mistake—don't come up with something outside of your sweet spot, because it's going to be harder to market. Focus on one core product or service, and market that one product or service on a consistent basis.

I want to remind you that you don't need to already be an expert in all aspects of your chosen business. You'll want to be an expert in the content of your product or your service, but you don't need to be an expert in everything else. You don't even have to be an expert on the method you choose to deliver that content. You can learn anything you need to know.

For example, I wasn't an expert on planning events, but I learned. If you want to offer a retreat, you don't need to take a whole class on planning retreats. However, it would be useful to go to a retreat and see how it's done. You can look at other retreats being offered in your industry, see how they're set up, and put your content into a similar format. This is something that you don't want to spend too much time on, or you'll hold yourself back.

Another mistake that entrepreneurs often make is to create five different products and services, and market all of them once in a while. When you have one main product or service, it's easier to have a consistent system where you can attract a steady stream of customers. Focus on one product or service now. You can add other things later.

I know you may have lots of ideas. If that's the case, I urge you to save them and offer them later. The goal here is to become known for a quality product or service in one area before branching out into others. The reputation you build with your first product or service will give people confidence in you and help you launch other products in the future.

To show you how this works, my first product was a course called The Personal Branding Boot Camp. This course guided people through a process to build their personal brand using a low-cost online marketing tool. I established my reputation as a trainer, speaker, and instructor with that product. After that, people followed me from course to course. When I offered my next product, The Blogging School, half of the people who had taken my Personal Branding Boot Camp signed up.

Eventually, I built a total of four courses, but I started with just one. To maximize your chances of success, I recommend that you do the same.

So, how do you figure out your signature product or service? We talked about making sure it was in your sweet spot, but you also want your signature product or service to focus on your ideal client. It has to be something that stirs your ideal client or customer. Otherwise, who's going to buy it? Go back to your homework on your ideal client and read it again. Look at what each ideal client struggles with and why she needs you. Your signature product or service should address a problem your ideal client wants to solve.

Possible Income Streams

Once you know what problem you're solving, you need to figure out what form your offering will take. Your ideas and concepts on their own can't make you money—you need to put them into a structure so that people can pay you for them. Here are 10 streams of income to give you some options for how to structure the business you create from your passion.

1. **Freelancing:** You can earn income by offering contracted services in a specific area such as photography, web/graphic design, personal styling, copywriting, editing, social media

management, or personal training. You can provide your services by the hour or in a package, depending on what you offer. As a freelance writer, I was paid a monthly fee for producing several articles per week for a career website.

2. **Consulting:** You can get paid generous fees for advising businesses, nonprofits, churches, and government agencies in your area of expertise. Consultants typically provide key deliverables as part of a time-bound contract, which usually runs for a few months to a year. As a nonprofit consultant, I maintained two long-term contracts with organizations that borrowed my brain and my time for 10 hours per week.

3. **Speaking:** You can build a lucrative stream of income as a keynote speaker or workshop leader for conferences all around the world. It's a great way to make a difference with your message AND get paid to travel. I've been a professional speaker since 2008, with more than 100 clients from New York to Nebraska who have paid me to teach, inspire, and motivate their audiences. I suggest you start by speaking for free at local events and attract paid gigs from there.

4. **Training:** You can earn a good living as a trainer for the staff or members of businesses, associations, nonprofits, churches, or government agencies. Training is usually done with a smaller group than you would speak for at a conference, which allows you go more in-depth with a 90-minute, half-day, or full-day session on a specific learning goal. As a trainer, I've worked with staff to get them up to speed on social media, show them how to manage millennial employees, and build their leadership skills in the workplace.

5. **Coaching:** You can help people all over the world through coaching in person, on the phone, or via Skype. The five most

popular areas are life, career, business, health, and relationship coaching. Most coaches either charge by the hour or create packages of sessions to help clients reach their goals over a period of one month or up to a year. As a life, career, and business coach I've helped clients change jobs, improve their lifestyles, switch careers, and build businesses doing what they love.

Coaching is an unregulated industry for the most part. Unless you get into health, legal, accounting, and other similar areas (which require certain licensing and certifications), you do not need certification to be a coach. Some training and expertise is recommended, but the best experience you can get in coaching people is to coach people. If people always tell you that you give great advice, or you help people find new jobs for free, then you're probably already a pretty good coach. You can definitely continue your education and training in the area, but you can begin coaching now. Just ensure that you choose a category or area of specialization as a coach.

Consulting is similar, and it's important to choose your consulting area of focus as well. There are numerous types of consulting, and you need to identify what "container" to put it in.

6. **Digital products and programs:** You can earn income by teaching what you know via teleseminars, webinars, home study programs, and audio/video trainings. I've been teaching online classes since 2010, when I was still an adjunct professor in D.C. What I found was that I could make a lot more money with my own courses than I ever would teaching part-time at a university. Once you establish yourself as an expert online, you can begin to offer your own courses on your areas of expertise. Setting up a blog and writing useful articles would be a great way to start building your audience.

A great example of a training product is an online video cooking class: You could include a recipe, an ingredients list, and then a video of you cooking the dish. It becomes more than a cooking class. It's a guide and a class, and then you can start an online forum to make it a total experience.

7. **Physical product:** You can add physical products to your business to earn additional income. Items like T-shirts, jewelry, mugs, purses, CDs, and DVDs are becoming easier and easier to sell due to advanced online technology. You can post your items on Etsy or eBay, and then ship them out when you receive orders. I've sold branded Happy Black Woman T-shirts and mugs through Zazzle over the past year. People love giving them as gifts! You could make jewelry, purses, or anything you have a passion for. Many of these products do not require a large financial investment.

8. **Books and eBooks:** You can create another income stream by adding books to your business in paperback, PDF, or Kindle format. I've self-published an eBook in PDF and Kindle formats and also a paperback. The paperback that I co-wrote in 2010 is still producing passive income with sales on Amazon.com. It's easier than ever to turn your writing into an eBook. The process is relatively simple, and the revenue potential is huge if you can build a following and a brand related to your book(s).

I recommend getting your feet wet with a low price point book to start. A lot of people hold onto books they've written for a long time, or they have books in their minds for years, afraid to release them until they're perfect. You really just need to get something out there. It's never going to be perfect. I've read famous authors' *New York Times* bestseller books and found typos. Don't wait until it's perfect—get it out there and make some money.

9. **Blogging:** You can earn money with your blog by participating in affiliate marketing, placing advertising on your site, or hosting sponsored posts. I've been blogging since 2007, and I've made hundreds of dollars in advertising income in my best traffic months. The downside to this income opportunity is that you need to post frequently and be getting a decent amount of traffic to your blog to really see some profit. It's not the best option for those just starting out, but the potential is huge for adding another income stream through your blog.

   There are many ways to monetize your blog, and we'll cover things like how much to charge and what commissions might be like. If you have a blogging topic that lends itself to sponsorships, affiliate relationships, or advertising and you can build up an audience, you can definitely monetize a blog. It can take time to build up a following, though, so this income stream is not the fastest way to begin earning revenue.

   You can also use your blog to promote other streams of income. A blog is just a website, so you can use it to sell your book or anything else. This is a great way to leverage that platform.

10. **Live events:** You may want to turn your ideas and concepts into live events like workshops, conferences, or retreats. Events can be a great way to attract your ideal client and to build a team. Experiment with different event formats. Women in business especially want live events, which provide opportunities to get together in person and build lifelong personal and business relationships.

    Events can be local or national in scope, from a three-hour workshop to a weeklong retreat. I held my first paid event back in 2011 as a weekend career training intensive that brought 11 attendees from all over the country. If you have valuable knowledge, resources, and tools to share, people will be excited to come and learn from you in person.

These are just 10 ways out of endless possibilities that will allow you to build streams of income. Write down your best guess or idea right now for your signature product or service. Be specific! It will likely fall into one of those 10 categories. If it's coaching, specify what kind and who your target market is.

Last year, I brought in 30% more revenue than I did the year before, all because I had multiple streams of income coming into my business. I highly recommend that you start with one signature product. Then, over time, incorporate more of these income streams into your business.

To give you a frame of reference, here are some examples of signature products and services from some of my past clients.

- My signature product and service is called *Wrapped in Pink*. My book is the product, and my service is speaking engagements where I also do a workshop.

- My signature service is live events. I just held a successful live event called Women on the Move on Women's Empowerment Network. It was uplifting and inspiring. I had a great turnout, and everyone's waiting for the next one. I now have a following, so I'm confident that I've found my sweet spot.

- The signature product or service for me is my speech, The 20th Mile. I'd love to do a keynote address or workshop on this, but I also have a lot of funny anecdotes and stories that I think would make a great eBook. They're about a marathon I ran, which was actually the Disney marathon. There's nothing like running 26.2 miles when you can stop and ride a roller coaster in the middle of the race, take pictures with Snow White, and stop in Germany so you can carry a beer across the finish line. It's the most unique experience. So that's really what I want to try to get across: that life is this really serious journey, but it can be fun and you can discover your character within.

I think the best idea for my signature is speaking on cultural competency. From that, I can promote my process improvement and gain clients that way. Process improvement consulting would be the signature service, and speaking is a marketing tool to attract people to it.

Pricing for Your Signature Product or Service

Once you decide on your signature product or service, you need to figure out how much to charge. I should warn you, pricing is tricky. Like everything else we're doing here, it's an art, not a science. No one has it all figured out, so you have to get comfortable testing and developing your price structure through trial and error. Start with your best guess. You can always adjust it later, either up or down. You can even double it later if you find that people are willing to pay that.

In my own experience, I learned that a low price does not necessarily mean high sales. In fact, often when I raised the price of a product, I got more sales. When your price is too low, many people have the perception that the quality of your product is also low. I learned that the hard way.

In my business, we really try to hit the sweet spot with our pricing. We want the price to be low enough to be attainable and make sure people get value from the event, but high enough that attendees value what they've purchased.

For your pricing, you don't need to do a whole bunch of market research. If you want to research your market, be smart about it. Do no more than 60 minutes of research online, and use that time to see what similar businesses are charging for the value they provide. The best way to see what value people provide is to purchase two or three products or services from some of your colleagues.

On the other hand, don't simply accept what you hear from others without performing your own investigation. Determine what is true for you. For example, when I was just getting started in speaking and coaching in the nonprofit industry, I heard that nonprofits don't have much money, so you can't charge very much. I found that to be untrue.

Some of my colleagues never charge for their speeches. When I was starting out, they warned me to be careful about asking for payment, because people might think I was in it for the money. My answer to that is: I am in it for the money. I'm a businessperson. That's what business is.

When I was starting out speaking and coaching, I checked out other people's speeches and workshops. I went to conferences as an attendee. I paid my way in, and I would go and see my colleagues speak—the ones I knew were getting paid. I looked at the value they were providing and what they charged.

I discovered that many people who speak for free will do their speech the night before, or they'll go on a panel and wing it. You can tell they're winging it, and they don't have any takeaways. On the other hand, my colleagues who were being compensated were prepared and professional. They had takeaways or handouts. They would have certain things that really raised the value of their talks. I started incorporating those things into my business to ensure that I was providing value for what I was charging.

Similarly, when I began coaching, I started getting coaching myself. I had a leadership coach, so I got a feel for what it was like to be a client.

Before your offer your first product or service, I encourage you to get out there and see what other people charge for similar products or services. If you're going to be a coach or anything that places you in front of an audience, I highly recommend attending similar talks, courses, or programs. If you're creating digital training or digital programs, purchase other similar products to get a sense of the market from a customer's perspective.

With events, there are endless options available to your ideal client. If you want to put on events, I highly recommend that you attend other events and see how other people are conducting them. Are people enjoying what they're getting? Are there good opportunities for networking that attendees are looking for?

If you want to do effective market research, go out there and be a client or an attendee. Be in the audience so you can see what kind of value your colleagues are providing. It's not enough to go to someone else's website and just copy their pricing structure. Please don't do that. The best way to establish pricing is to be a client, but I'm going to list some guidelines on pricing that come from a range of industries and from what I've observed.

When you're first starting out, it's really important to state your prices on your marketing materials, especially if it's a product or service with a fixed price. It's a no-brainer. If you're selling a T-shirt, you need to tell people how much the T-shirt costs. If your prices vary, you can always give a price range.

When I was researching web designers for a custom site design for happyblackwoman.com, I collected quotes from different designers. This is known as doing your due diligence. Some companies didn't have any price ranges on their sites, but the one I hired had a range. It said: "Our custom designed websites start at $3,000."

First of all, you can quickly see that they're at the high end of web design and they'll probably do a great job, and that you need to have at least $3,000 to use their services. The worst thing you can do when you're first starting out is to attract the wrong customers. Over time, your reputation will precede you. My web designers are making a name for themselves. They're not a low-budget web designer, and they're not going to be known for that. They've set their process accordingly.

Many people hesitate about this, but at some point, you have to put a price out there. Tell people what it is and let them decide if they want to pay it or not. Don't give them the runaround.

By being clear on your pricing, you let people know whether you're in their budget or not. This is particularly important in the nonprofit industry. Many organizers think you'll speak for free because you're an expert and you just want to give. My response to this is that I'm a professional speaker and here are my prices. If you don't have a budget to compensate me in full for what I do, then you'd be better off finding another speaker.

Because I'm clear on my prices up front, the people who call me are the right people. They already know how much I charge, so they're asking me if I'm available for their conference and not to speak for free. That's really a great place to be.

I'm going to give you some guidelines that you can use for pricing. Again, there are exceptions to every rule in business, but I want to give you an idea of the low end for some of these streams of income. (Only you know what your high end might be.) When you set your prices, at least charge the minimum given. Don't go any lower. Otherwise, you don't appear professional. Prospective clients may think: Does this person know how to run a business? Why is she not charging enough to cover the cost for her time?

These are just some rough numbers based on what I've seen in a lot of these areas:

- **Freelancing:** There can be come variation based on the service offered, but $50 to $300 an hour is standard and really common. So if you're acting as a social media manager or virtual assistant and you're really good at it and providing value, I've seen $50 and up. The great thing about charging appropriately for your freelance work is that if a client purchases a package or multiple hours, you can offer a discount. At least you are discounting from a very good original rate.

- **Photography:** I've never seen a photographer charge less than about $150 an hour for headshots or anything else.

- **Consulting:** This can vary by industry, but I've never seen a consultant who charges less than $100 an hour. If you're still charging $25, $35, or $50 an hour, you need to increase it. When you're a consultant, you are perceived as an expert, and experts get paid for their expertise. You invested thousands of dollars to get the expertise that you have to be a consultant. That's what your client is paying for, and he or she is receiving value from your investment. This really applies to any kind of service, by the way. The value you provide is not just in your time, but also in what you had to invest to be able to provide that value. So charge an hourly rate for consulting of $100 to $500 an hour.

- **Speaking:** Anyone who has invested time and money in training and experience to become a speaker should not be charging less than $500. Anything less than $500 is an honorarium (like a small stipend), not a real fee. If you have to travel, you need to charge more. I've seen up to $10,000 charged for a keynote speech, and for corporate speeches it can increase astronomically. $500 to $10,000 is a big range for a speaking engagement fee, but it depends on the industry and the size of the conference. If it's a large conference and attendees are paying $1,000 a head to be there, the organizers have the money to compensate you well. If it's going to be a room of 1,000 attendees, that's a lot of value you're going to provide to a lot of people.

- **Training:** I've never found a trainer who charges less than $1,000 for a workshop, and it can be as high as $20,000 for a series. We had a trainer and consultant do a series of workshops for our organization that came out to $20,000. Even in the nonprofit industry rates are high, with corporate training being even higher.

An excellent strategy to increase your earnings as a trainer or a speaker is to book a series. So if you want to hold a leadership workshop, don't pitch the organizer on just the one workshop. Propose that you hold one workshop for $2,000, or a series of three over six months. Offer a discount of $1,000 if they book the series, making it $5,000 for the three workshops. You earn more money in total that way, and they get more value. It's a win/win.

- **Coaching:** I've never had a coach who charged less than $100 an hour. The only time I provided coaching for less than that was for nonprofit individuals, and I was trying to help people who needed it. Unfortunately, it was a nightmare. People consistently missed their appointments and generally didn't value the service they were getting for less than $100 an hour, so I had to start charging more.

I realized that people needed to understand the value of my services, and I started adding more value too. My clients receive worksheets, plans to follow, and forms to fill out even when we're not on the phone working together. So the range for coaching is $100 to $500 an hour in any level of business or executive coaching. In corporate coaching, that can increase exponentially. Once again, if these rates make you hyperventilate, you can start at the low end with $100 an hour.

You can also increase your income by offering packages, and I'll give you some sense of the common rates. Once I had raised my price to at least the minimum, my first package was priced at $400 for a month of coaching. I talk to people once a week, so four times a month at $100 was an easy calculation. So at the low end, this is how you can start. Depending on your confidence level, you really should charge more, but if you feel overly anxious charging $500 an hour, your fear will stop you from marketing yourself. When you determine your prices, you'll need to set a fee that is sufficient, but also one that you feel comfortable with.

- **Digital products and programs:** Digital products range in price from $97 to $997 dollars. You will likely need to adjust and re-adjust your pricing on these because when it comes to products, people really do have a tendency to be focused on getting the lowest price possible.

  You've likely noticed in many stores that items are rarely priced at $30, but rather $29.97, for example. Large companies know that psychologically we think we're paying less when we see prices ending in 3, 7, 9, and 5. While this may seem pointless when the customer is saving very little with this type of pricing, it's in line with human nature. If you can help a customer make a decision by saving him or her three dollars or three cents, I would suggest that you do. Digital products and programs (including online training) in the personal development and training industry are priced around $97. You can increase the price for more specialized items like teaching people how to do something very technical, but this is generally a good range to be in.

- **Physical products:** Pricing on tangible products depends greatly on the product itself. In general, it's probably not worth your time to sell anything lower than about $9.99. The price range really varies with physical products, but the most important consideration is to ensure that you cover all of your costs for materials and time, as well as earn some profit on each sale.

- **Books and eBooks:** Kindle eBooks are priced as low as $2.99. The point of creating eBooks is not really to get rich, although that is possible. You can sell a lot of Kindle eBooks, especially if you're writing fiction. When you get into physical books, especially books that come with a specialized workbook as with instructional workbooks, you can charge more because that book or workbook contains specialized knowledge. So there's some wiggle room in this area, and I suggest looking at what's out there and the price range to be in.

One way to raise the price on books and eBooks is to call yours a "guide." Then it becomes more like a digital product or program and you can charge more. I had a client who wanted to sell a book of recipes to help people go vegan. We decided to market it as a guide and included a book of recipes, a shopping list of what you need for your pantry, substitutions for vegan eating, as well as some instructional videos and additional guides. So it became more than a book or eBook. It became a guide, and we could charge more money for it.

- **Blogging:** We've covered this to some degree, but there are a few more things you should know. When you do advertising on your blog, it's likely going to be earning cents per click. Each time a person clicks on the ad on your blog, you earn a few cents. If you're doing affiliate marketing, that becomes dollars per commission, so it can definitely bring in more revenue. For example, let's say you have a fashion blog and you want to promote a certain designer's clothing. If this designer has an affiliate program like a referral program and you sell one of his or her shirts on your blog, you'll earn a few dollars' commission. That is definitely more profitable than earning cents per click for advertising.

You can also earn revenue through sponsored posts. If you do that, I suggest you accept no less than $50 per post. In all of the blogging I've done, I've only had one sponsored post. It was a $50 post that I ran as a test to see how much work went into it. Personally, I'd rather write my own posts and promote my own programs, but if you want to build your blog, accepting sponsored posts is an option. If you have a travel blog, you could do a sponsored post in which you do a review of a hotel. You'll get a free night in a hotel, and you get paid for writing the post about it. Depending on the subject of your blog, there are other variations of this that could help you to monetize your blog.

- **Live events:** When calculating ticket pricing for events, you need to consider a lot of hard costs as well as paying yourself. Anywhere from $47 to $3,000 for a ticket is pretty standard. The event could be two hours long or a multi-day event like my Launch Your Business Boot Camp. Obviously, the duration of the event will affect your pricing, in combination with the value you're offering. If it's just a random networking event, the value may be lower than a networking event that includes some training and a special VIP meal. Set your ticket pricing accordingly.

How to Set Prices

The goal in pricing is to implement value-based pricing. We've covered some guidelines already, but it's also important to set your pricing according to value. Prices should not be based solely on your time invested. Even when you charge by the hour, you're not just charging for your time, but the value you're providing in that hour.

For example, if you're a coach and you work with someone for an hour, and in that hour she has a breakthrough that changes her entire life, that is priceless. That's a lot of value you just gave her. So pricing is not just based on your time, but on the value provided. But at the very minimum, pricing should include the cost of your time, any materials, overhead, and travel. It's crucial that you include all of the costs that go into your product or service.

We covered how you can earn higher fees by offering packages and bundles of services. This also applies if you're selling physical products.

You can offer a bundle of products at a small discount, or bulk pricing on orders of 50 books or more, for example. Bundling can bring more sales for you and more value for your client.

When you're talking about your pricing, use words like "investment" instead of "cost" or "fee." Thinking of something as a "cost" or "fee" because makes the price sound high, when it's actually an investment. For example, when people buy coaching from me, it's an investment in themselves and the goals they want to achieve. When you're talking to a company or organization about hiring you as a teacher or consultant, it's an investment in their staff and company knowledge base. It's an investment in the long-term growth and health of their organization. It's not a cost or a fee.

Some people may want to hire you or buy your product or service, but they don't have sufficient money at that moment. There are options to ensure that you still make the sale: You can offer discounts to get the sale now instead of later; you can offer your clients and customers payment plans; and you can give potential customers a way to pay in installments.

You can also offer what I call "fast action savings" or "quick decision savings." Give potential clients an incentive to decide right now. For example, when I talk to a client on the phone and she wants to do coaching but doesn't have all the money on hand, I say, "Well, if you decide to hire me within 48 hours, I'll give you a discount of a couple hundred dollars." People usually agree to proceed, and somehow they end up finding the money.

People want to get the best price possible. If my offering a discount is going to help them decide to go after their goal with my help, then it's worth it for both of us.

Other types of discounts can also boost your sales. Offering early bird discounts, especially when it comes to events, pushes people to make a decision. If there's no incentive to decide right now, people will put it off, and later becomes never. Paid-in-full discounts are also effective, where a lower total price is offered if the client pays for a course or event in full as opposed to making payments.

You can also do seasonal sales to boost your cash flow. You can do this for any of your products or services, and people love a good sale.

At this point, I'd like you to identify the pricing for your signature product or service. I want you to identify the low point and the high point. So, what is the lowest price you should charge for your product or service, and what is the highest, even if the high point seems unrealistic right now? Based on those two numbers, what do you actually plan to charge?

Here are a few examples from past clients.

- This is something I really struggled with. My target is high net worth, but right now, I only have an hourly rate that I charge. My business is lifestyle management. Basically my clients give me their to-do lists, which could include anything from grocery shopping to event planning to planning a vacation. After going through this material, I'm thinking about offering packages. Right now, my low rate is $40, but I'm thinking ideally it should be probably closer to $75. That would be on the high end.

- Well, after going through this book and doing the homework assignments, I've decided that my high for speaking engagements would be $2,000, and my low would be $500. The $500 would be the honorarium for organizations that really could not afford to pay over $500.

Again, the great thing about having a high and low is that you can negotiate with them. It's not a hard and fast thing—you can negotiate within the relationship that you have with the client organization. But as long as you know your low, you don't want to go below that, and that will help you.

Creating Your Sales Page

Many people are intimidated by selling, but creating a sales page can be easy once you know the elements that should go in it. Basically, there are a few questions that you need to answer. Once you've done that, you can put your product or service on your website, on a brochure, or on a flyer, and people will be able to understand what you have to offer. This is called your sales page, and you use this to promote your product or service.

You can think of this as if you're making a flyer that you want to hand out at an event. At the top, you want to have the name of your product, service, or package. So let's say you're going to a conference where there will be entrepreneurs who need personal and administrative help. Perhaps you offer a "Give me your to-do list" package. Your flyer should then go on to describe what it is and what's included. If there's a picture you can add, like a picture of a to-do list, then that would be really powerful.

Let's say that this package will help you if you feel like there are more items on your to-do list than there are hours in the day, and what's included is six hours of personal assistance. You'll want to include this information on the flyer, and then describe the benefits of the service for your client. What's so great about it, and how will it help them? Go back to the language that you used for your ideal client profile—the struggle. If your ideal client is struggling with having insufficient time for her family, or her packed schedule is causing her stress, then you know that those are the benefits you can provide. Explain that this package will help them free up time to use for something that they actually want to do. Also be sure to list the price, or at least a price range, for the service or product.

Then make the call to action. Be clear about how they can purchase your product, service, or package. Personally, I get frustrated when I get a flyer with information but little or no instruction on how to proceed. You want to tell potential clients how to get started. If they can purchase through your website, make those instructions clear and easy. If you're coaching, then direct them to an online application form. Perhaps you just have a telephone number and e-mail address to contact if they're interested. Whatever you'd like interested customers to do, make that clear. A call to action is essential.

The sales page is part of your homework for this chapter; you're going to work on that for your signature product or service. Writing your sales page is a big step toward building a business that earns money. You also need to make sure the rest of the business is set up and ready to receive money. That's what we'll cover next.

Ready to Receive Checklist

This checklist is really a listing of the basic tools that most entrepreneurs need to start getting paid in their business. As you read through it, check off the tools you already have in place and make a plan to get the ones you're missing.

This checklist can be really inspiring, because it gives you an idea of what you've already accomplished, as well as what you still need to do. I call it "ready to receive." Many of us, especially new entrepreneurs, have a lot of ideas and great concepts—but nothing that can actually be sold. When someone approaches you in a grocery store and says she heard about your business and wants to hire you, or you have a great conversation at a conference with someone who is interested in your work, will you be ready? When someone says, "I want to work with you. Here's my credit card. I'm ready," are you ready to receive that client or customer?

If you're missing some of the items on this list, you may not feel ready. When you don't feel ready, you also don't tend to market yourself. You don't go out and promote your website. You don't put articles on your blog. You don't go to networking events, because you don't feel like you're ready. So I want you to be ready to receive clients who want to work with you. Depending on the rules in your area, here's what you'll need:

- **Business entity:** You need to have some type of business entity. I'm not a lawyer or a CPA, so I can't advise you on this, but you do need to figure out what kind of business entity you will use for your business.

  Most businesses in the 10 income streams we covered are set up as either a sole proprietor or a limited liability company (LLC). I was a sole proprietor for six years, and I became an LLC last year. You don't have to start right out being an LLC or corporation.

  Setting up a business entity is something you should research on your own, and the type may be dependent on where you live. Don't worry about this; just take care of it. Once you know what you need, you can take steps to get it.

- **Business license and/or permits:** You likely need some kind of business license. Depending what you're offering, you may also need a permit.

  For most of the income streams in this book, you won't need a permit. The exception may be if you're a personal trainer and people are coming to your house for training, or anything of that nature. Whether you need any permits depends on your location and your industry, so check the regulations for your area.

For most businesses, you just need a basic license. You pay a small fee, do the paperwork, and you're done. You will need a business address, but for a lot of people, that's simply their home address. Some people choose to get a PO Box, and that's fine too.

- **Business bank account:** A business bank account can be really helpful to separate your expenses and your income, especially when tax time arrives. Again, I'm not a tax professional, but I've had my own nightmares related to banking and taxes. It really helps to have a separate bank account. A PayPal business account is also really helpful when you want people to pay you with a credit card. I use Payflow Pro with enhanced billing, which allows me to offer payment plans. If you have a basic PayPal account, a payment plan is going to be a nightmare because you have to manage the payments yourself. Payflow Pro allows you to set up automatic withdrawal of customer payments from their accounts.

- **Cash box:** If you're selling items at a vendor table, then you need to have a cash box for in-person cash transactions. Honestly, a cash box or a cash bag is a basic necessity in this scenario. It's unprofessional to stuff a customer's payment in your pocket or purse. Invest in an inexpensive cash box.

- **Square or PayPal credit card swipe app:** If you want to accept credit cards, another very useful tool is a credit card swipe app. There's an app called Square with a little reader that you stick into your smart phone or iPad, and you can swipe people's credit cards. It works pretty well. Another option is PayPal Here, which works with your iPad.

- **EIN:** An EIN is a number you can request if you don't want to use your Social Security number for your business. As a sole proprietor for years, I just used my Social Security number and that worked fine, but you can get an EIN if you prefer. Also, in many jurisdictions, you need an EIN to get a business bank account. If this is the case, you can get one almost instantly by calling the IRS during business hours. It's very easy to get one. If your client is an organization, they'll want your EIN so they can send you a 1099 at the end of the year.

- **W-9 forms:** If you're working with clients like organizations, you'll probably need W-9 forms. Many organizations will request that you fill out a W-9 form with your name, address, and Social Security number or EIN.

- **Website:** You need a website for your business, which we'll go over in Chapter Four. If you don't have a website yet, start now and improve it later. At the very least, make a basic flyer or brochure so that wherever you go, you have something that describes your product or service. Don't be daunted because you don't have a website. Just make a stack of flyers and give one to everyone you meet. And then have a plan to get your website up.

- **Forms:** Depending what you're selling, you may need order forms, contracts, or agreement forms. If you're selling speaking or other services, I recommend having some kind of contract or agreement form. I have an agreement form I give to my clients that details what they've agreed to pay me for coming to speak at their event, the event date and time, and that they agree to pay for my travel. These forms don't need to be elaborate, and there are plenty of cheap or free templates on the Internet. If you have the budget for it, you can hire a lawyer and have him or her draft something for you, but in most cases this isn't necessary.

- **Bookkeeping system:** This is something that can become important down the line once you start bringing in more revenue. QuickBooks is the gold standard, but GoDaddy Bookkeeping is also a great program that pulls in all your expenses and costs for around $10 a month. I used that for years until I hired a bookkeeper.

These are just some of the things that you'll likely need in order to get paid in your business and to start bringing in more revenue. If you have some of these things, you're already ready to receive. But once you get everything you need, you'll be even more confident and determined.

If you don't have everything right now, that's OK. For example, if you still need a business bank account, just put that on your to-do list. Get that set up, and everything will be much easier.

Adding it Up

To conclude this chapter, I'd like to leave you with this thought: When you look at your pricing, you're going to see that your prices need to be at a certain level to reach your income goal. This means that you're going to have to provide a certain level of value to match that. If you want to earn a certain amount of money per year, you can. You just need to offer packages with a lot of value, commit yourself to marketing on a consistent basis, and get those clients.

Looking ahead to Chapter Four, we'll be working on creating or improving your website, as well as continuing in the process of gaining clarity and setting up a structure for your passion, your expertise, and your sweet spot.

If you're not 100 percent clear on your business yet, I don't want you to feel bad. Every chapter in this book will help you get closer and closer to knowing what you're doing.

It's important to note that even after you launch a business, things change. They shift, and that's okay. It's a process. It may be hard to see that right now, but it's true. When you put yourself out there, you start getting feedback and information from your clients, and you'll shift your business based on what you're hearing. That's business. But you have to start somewhere. Our current goal is to help you get to a place where you feel comfortable putting your product or service out there. The next chapter will be a great step in that process.

Homework

This chapter covers a lot, and I know that you're probably feeling overwhelmed right now with information and ideas. Hopefully you're ready to get started on your homework, which for Chapter Three is to create or improve your sales page to include your pricing structure.

1. What will your signature product or service be? Which income stream will it be based on?

2. What are the low and high price points for your signature product or service? What will be your initial price for it?

3. Create the sales page for your signature product or service. Be sure to include the answers to these questions:

    a. What is the name of the product, service, or package?

    b. What picture(s) can you add to capture attention and make it clear what you're offering?

    c. What are you offering in this product, service, or package?

    d. Which of your ideal client's struggles or problems does this package address?

    e. What are the benefits? (How will it help the buyer?)

    f. What's the price (or price range)?

    g. What's the call to action? (What does the reader need to do to buy this product, service, or package?)

4. Complete the 'ready to receive' checklist. Which items do you still need in order to get started in your business? Make a plan to get these things set up.

CHAPTER 4: GET ONLINE

This chapter is all about creating an online presence for your business, whether you need to create your website from scratch or simply improve it. When people ask you "Where can I go to find out more about you and your work?", you'll have an answer you can be proud of.

It doesn't help your business when you tell people that your website is under construction. Instead, I want you to start by setting up a basic website. You can improve it later, but for now you just need a page where people can go and learn more about you, what you do, what you offer, and how to contact you.

In this chapter, you'll learn the fastest, cheapest, and easiest way to set up a website for your business. It's not the perfect way, but it is the best way to get an online presence quickly. I'll go over the three essential pages you must have on your site in order to be profitable. Many people think that you need a whole bunch of perfect pages on your website, but you really don't. As discussed in Chapter Three, our goal is to get your business ready to receive clients. That's it. We're not trying to win any awards for your website.

You'll notice that this chapter continues with the work you did in Chapter Three around getting paid. We're going to put all of those details you put together for your signature product or service onto your website.

We'll also cover how to tell your story so that your website draws others to you and your business. This is one of the ways you'll attract your ideal client. I'll also share what you should include on your website to position yourself as someone who can be trusted.

Creating Your Website

It's essential that you understand and accept that in 2015, every business should have a website. Clients simply expect you to have an online presence. A website makes it much easier for people to learn about you and to share that information with their friends. The easiest, most economical way to do this is to set up a website using simple blogging software.

You may think you need to hire an expensive web designer to build your website. If you have the budget to hire a web designer, by all means, do that. However, it isn't necessary. I had a basic blogging site for years, and it still allowed me to receive clients.

The fact is, you don't have to have a fancy website in order to receive clients. You just need to have a place online that has all the information that people need to hire you. For many people, their website is essentially an online brochure. Of course, you can always improve it as you go along, but right now, the focus is making sure that you have some type of online presence.

If you already have a website, you can use this chapter to improve your site. But if you have no online presence yet, this chapter will help you create one.

Choosing a Name

The first step is to choose a name for your site. It's important that you don't allow indecision at this stage to postpone creating your online presence.

I was talking to a coaching client the other day about the process of setting up her website. She said, "Well, you know, I don't know what to call it. I guess I'll put that on hold." We're not in the business of putting things on hold. We want to see how we can move forward in the fastest possible way. So we decided that she would use her name for her site and if she thought up a different name for her website in the future, she could just change it. The goal is to get you up and running *right now*.

You have two options for naming your website:

- You can use your own name, as in first and last name.com, which is what I recommend. I had RosettaThurman.com for many, many years, and then I created my new business and changed it to happyblackwoman.com. Changing your website name is not difficult, and your old site name can be set up to redirect visitors to your new site.

- You can also use your own name and a tagline, or you can craft a snazzy name—something creative that fits with the focus of your business. But again, I must caution you not to be too elaborate with the name of your website. When you're at a networking event or if you're telling someone how to get to your site, you don't want it to be complicated. For example, RosettaThurmanConsultantForWomenAroundTheWorld.com is simply too long.

The best thing to do is to make it easy for people to find you. For most people, the easiest thing to do is to use yourname.com. It's better to use .com instead of .net or .org because more people are familiar with .com domains. You can say it very easily on the radio, or as you're speaking from the stage. If you use .org or .net, people will automatically go to the .com version of your site, and they might not be able to find you.

You'll need to purchase your domain name, which you can arrange through your hosting service. You may have heard of GoDaddy. com, where you can also buy domain names. Bluehost.com is what I recommend because I've been using them since 2008 to host my websites, but there are many other hosting providers. The key here is that you purchase your domain name and host your site so that people can get to your website.

The beauty of all of this is that you can always change it later. This is just something to get you up and running.

When I first started out in 2007, I had an ugly little blog. I didn't know anything about blogging, and I didn't have any training in it. Blogging was still a relatively new social platform in 2007, so I was just looking at other people's blogs and seeing what they were doing and how they were setting things up.

Two years later, people were asking me to teach them about blogging. Even though my blog was ugly at first, people could see and respect the hands-on experience I gained from running it. As clients, people want to see the fruits of your labor. They don't want to see that you've had a lot of training and no experience. I'm sure you wouldn't want to go to a doctor who's had a lot of training but has never performed any procedures. You want both.

So, don't be intimidated. The training that you're getting right now is going to be sufficient to get your site up and running with blogging software. Basically, you have two options: Set up your site for free or self-host your website using wordpress.org.

Self-hosting is the gold standard for a business website. Every business should eventually self-host its own website. Among other things, it provides more options for customization—more options for plugins and widgets make your site look sharp and professional. But again, this is not a requirement. It's something that many people work up to.

I started out with a free website on blogger.com, and I didn't self-host until a year and a half later. Once again, start now and improve later.

Free Hosting

The cheapest way to get your website set up quickly is to set it up for free using a blogging platform like wordpress.com or blogger.com. All you have to do is go to one of those websites and set up your site. The site will ask you what you want to call your website, and you enter the name you've chosen. You will choose a password and user name, and you'll be set up within five minutes. There are different templates you can choose from, among other things, but at the basic level, you set up your account and your site is ready to go right away.

Out of those two options (wordpress.com and blogger.com), WordPress is the better choice, because they have more design options. If you want to host your blog for free, I recommend WordPress.

Within the first five minutes of this chapter, you've learned how to get your website up and running, so that's exciting. Now you can set up your website for free, which is an excellent start. Or, you can get even more design options and technical support with a paid hosting plan.

Paid Hosting

To get started, you need to buy your domain name. You can do this through various hosting providers, but I prefer Bluehost. You can go to Bluehost.com and set up an account; pay your hosting fee for one, two, or three years; and get your site set up that way. When you purchase a hosting plan with Bluehost, you can just call them and they'll walk you through setting it all up. If you use a free site, there really isn't much support because it's a free service.

In addition, a paid hosting plan gives you more customization options. For example, you can purchase a template from any site on the internet and upload it to make your website look however you want it to. You're not limited.

If you don't have those skills and you don't want to learn, then going with a free site on wordpress.com might be your best bet. If you do want to self-host your site, you can use your .com domain name and get your hosting plan set up.

Your Plan

When I work with my clients on getting their online presence going, we always have a basic plan and a long-term plan. Because they're just starting out and don't have a budget for a website yet, the basic plan for them is to set up a free website. The long-term plan is to get a custom-designed site within the next year.

You can have that same kind of plan for yourself so you don't have to wait. If you're not ready to self-host or you don't have the budget to pay for the hosting plan, I recommend that you set up a free website using wordpress.com.

Many people mistakenly think that they have to wait until they have the money for a custom-designed website because they want to look fancy. What you want to do is put your free website up first and start getting some interest and buzz. Then, as you start making money in your business over the course of the following year, you can put aside some money to hire a web designer. The next year, you can make a big splash and announce your new website. That's far better than the alternative: waiting through a year of missed opportunities because you don't have a site at all.

As long as you have the essential three pages on your site, you can attract clients and people will know what you do. The design doesn't really matter. I have to keep reminding people that most of their clients are not going to be tech savvy enough to know what a good website even looks like anyway, so just having the basics is going to be enough.

What to Put on the Site

It's essential that you have the right information on your website so that people don't leave the site without knowing what you offer. This is where you make it very clear what products or services you provide. You don't have to have a page for each of your services right now, especially as you're trying to figure out what services you're going to offer or what products you're going to sell. One page on what you're offering is enough for now.

When I was just starting out, I had a page that said 'Hire Me.' It listed the types of speaking engagements that I did and workshops that I conducted. Over the years, my website has become more sophisticated. Now I'm passing these lessons on to you so that you can be pretty sophisticated right off the bat.

The Three Essential Pages

Here are the three pages you must have on your website—the basic pages. You can have more pages than this, but for the minimum effective website, you must have an 'About' page, a page about your services and/or products, and a 'Contact' page. Basically, you want people to be able to figure out who you are, what you're about, what you're offering or selling, and how they can contact you.

It blows my mind when I see professionally designed websites that don't even have a proper contact page. You go through the site and you're interested in their services, but there's no contact information—no e-mail address, no phone number. They've put all of their information out there, but it seems like they're still not ready to receive clients.

These three pages will help you get ready to receive because people will now have all the information they need to make a decision about hiring you. At the very least, they have your contact information if they want to call or e-mail you to explore a potential relationship.

- 'About' page: This page is for information about you. This will be the most viewed page on your site. People are nosy. They want to know who's behind this business. If there's very little information there or it seems like you're hiding, people are not going to trust you.

- 'Services and Products' page: This is where your sales page is going to go. In the homework from Chapter Three, you created a sales page for your signature product or service, identifying what it is, the benefit, how much it costs, what's included, and how people can take the next step. That will become your 'Services and Products' page for your website.

- 'Contact' page: This page must have information about how people can contact you. Later in this chapter, I'll give you the language to use for this page.

For now, I want to discuss each of these pages in a little more detail.

'About' Page

Your 'About' page should have your bio and your story, along with a good head shot. Many women get cold feet about putting their picture online, but in order to build your business and attract customers, you have to get people to know, like, and trust you. Giving a face and a name to your business helps them to know, like, and trust you. Your 'About' page should tell people why you do what you do and make people eager to work with you.

In my background in fundraising, we were always looking for people who fit LAI: people with a Link, an Ability, and an Interest in working with our organization. One of the ways to do that is to instill trust, so on your website you want to have pictures of the people who are doing the work. The business is you, so you must have a picture of you with a smile on your face.

It doesn't have to be professionally taken, but you can get professionally done head shots in most cities for under $300. I got the photos I have on my site now done in D.C. for about $250. Or, you can always put on a favorite outfit and get a friend or family member to take you outside on a nice, sunny day and take a picture of you.

Don't use the lack of a photo as an excuse for not writing your 'About' page. Get one, or pick the one you have that you like the best. Then challenge yourself to swap it out with a better one within the next few weeks.

There are lots of options for naming your 'About' page. You can call it 'About,' 'About Me,' or 'About *Your Name.*' So I could say 'About Rosetta,' or I could make it a question: 'Who Is Rosetta?' You can also use 'Meet *Your Name.*' Choose the one that resonates the most with you.

Along with your picture, you also need a bio. Many people don't have a bio, even though this is a basic marketing tool for yourself and for your business. If you have a LinkedIn profile, you'll need a bio to put in the summary section. We'll talk more about social media in Chapter Five, but your bio can be used for so many different purposes that you really should have one, even if it's just a couple of sentences about you.

Some people don't like to talk about themselves, but if you want a business, you're going to have to talk about yourself at some point. Expecting people to know and understand you, your expertise, your experience, and what you have to offer without your help is placing too heavy a burden on your potential client. Creating a bio doesn't have to be intimidating; I'll walk you through it in this section.

To begin your bio, start with your 'What I Do' statement. Then add in any expertise, credentials, or experience you have.

In some cases, your credentials are not education or training. Your credentials can be the number of years of experience you have in your industry, the type of expertise you've developed through your work, or the positions that you've held. For example, I was in Denver today to speak at a nonprofit conference because I have over 10 years of experience in that industry. I don't work in the industry now, but I have a lot of knowledge about it, I have a lot of experience in it, and I can relate to that audience. You don't have to have formal education on your subject matter; you can talk about your experience, your expertise, and any other credentials you may have.

Your bio should also include why you started your business. People like to know some part of your story, even if it's very brief. You don't have to go into your whole life story of where you were born and where you grew up and all of that, although you can if you want to, if you think that would be interesting for your ideal client. Especially in coaching, people love stories. Because there are so many coaches to choose from, clients often read numerous websites and choose a coach because his or her story is similar to their own.

I had a client who wanted to coach unwed mothers, and her whole bio was really about her experience being a single mother herself. Let's face it: If you're a single mom and you want some support on that journey, you're probably going to want someone who has been there. That's the benefit of sharing something personal; it's up to you how personal to get.

Your bio can be written in first or third person. It may help you to write it in third person and then decide if you want to get more informal.

Here are some examples for how to write a great bio. I'll use the example of Gina Smitt. Starting with her 'What I Do' statement, this is just a quick example of what her bio might look like:

Gina Smitt is a marketing consultant who provides social media training for artists who want to expand their businesses so that they can change the world with their art. Gina has six years of marketing experience, a bachelor's degree in Digital Media, and has worked on a social media campaign.

It's very clear what Gina Smitt does, who she does it for, her ideal clients, and how her services can help them. Then she lists her credentials.

If you don't have formal education, it doesn't matter. If you had any formal education you can put it down there.

For example, in my bio I wrote that I have a bachelor's degree in English. I also included my master's degree in Organizational Management, which appeals to some people because many think that English majors can't create a profitable career or business—all we know how to do is write.

Don't discount your education or experience just because it may not be directly related to what you want to do in your business. Some of the things you've done in the past show your leadership and your ability to be creative. Be sure to include any relevant volunteer work you've done, or committees and boards that you have served on.

Next, you'll want to include part of your personal story. This is just something very basic I made up for our marketing consultant, Gina Smitt:

She started her business after meeting so many artists who were struggling with their marketing.

Your experience might be that you wanted to start this business because you have a burning passion for X, Y, and Z, and you decided to help people with this area—with this service or product—and you want to share with people what you do in your free time. An easy way to share something personal about yourself is by saying "In her free time…"

and then filling in the rest. This can help people find something in your bio to connect with.

So for Gina:

In her free time she enjoys baking cupcakes while her husband, Jeremy, watches football.

So now you know that Gina likes baking, she has a husband, and he likes football. If you have one or more of those things in common, you may start to feel a connection with Gina.

I've had many iterations of my bio, and it's funny the things that people connect with. I have in my bio now that I like a big Mai Tai. To some people, that shows that I'm not uptight—that I can be fun and like to let loose and have a good time. You may want to put something in your bio that lets people know certain things about you as well.

'Services and Products' Page

The second page you must have is a 'Services and Products' page. As I mentioned earlier, your sales page can serve as the content for this page.

The whole point of the 'Services and Products' page is to describe your services and/or your products. It's essential that you put this information on your site so that people know you're a business and that you have products and services for sale.

I often hear from new clients that people are always asking them to do things for free. My response is that your website doesn't really say that you charge money for your services, so maybe if we update your site and add some language around that, people will realize that you are an actual business and not just someone who likes doing a website for praise and recognition. Posting at least a price range is definitely something that lets people know that you're serious.

Your 'Services and Products' page should not be just a list of bullet points. "I do consulting, speaking, and coaching" is really not enough. Give your potential clients some detail on what those services include, as well as some prices or price ranges.

Then, you want to guide people to the next action step. Show them how they can purchase, register, sign up, or learn more. You must have a call to action. If you have a great page about your services (including your prices or your price ranges), but then there's nothing at the bottom of the page to tell people how they can actually purchase or learn more, the information is all wasted. You have to give people a way forward if they want to invest in your services or buy your product.

Here are some calls to action that you can put on your website, and they're very simple:

- Buy now

- Register here

- Click to learn more

- Fill out this form to sign up for a free consultation.

You really have to tell people exactly what to do. Label your pages, your links, and your buttons so that people can just click and then purchase. Not everyone is going to purchase from your website, but it's wise to make it easy for people who want to.

There are a variety of options for naming your services and products page. You can call it 'Services,' 'Products,' or 'Programs' depending on the type of business you have. Again, if you have just one kind of service that you're offering right now and you're not sure where to go with it, you can put up a 'Hire Me' page to let people know that they can work with you for a fee. That's how I started out: I put a 'Hire Me' page on my ugly little blog, and people knew that I was for hire but didn't do things for free.

Another option is to call your page 'Work with Me.' That's very clear. People who want to work with you further know that there's probably going to be an additional fee for working with you directly. This is especially applicable when it comes to services.

You can be specific on your services or products page: call it 'Coaching,' 'Get Coaching,' 'Training,' 'Consulting,' or 'Speaking' if that's your signature product or service. You can be even more direct and name your page 'Book Me to Speak' or 'Book Anita to Speak,' and include all the information about your speaking and pricing on that page.

If you have a book or a physical product, you can be very direct and name that page 'Buy My Book.' If you have several items that you have for sale such as branded T-shirts or mugs or things like that, you can name it 'Shop' so it's like you have a little shop on your website. Those are just a few ideas for how to name your page.

'Contact' Page

The third page you need to have on your website is a 'Contact' page. A proper 'Contact' page should include your full name. Going back to the 'know, like, and trust' factor of being a business owner, people need to trust you, so you should put your full name on the page. You're asking people to give you their money. They want to give their money to someone who can at least give them her full name. If I'm going to pay you with my PayPal account and my credit card, I at least need to know who you are.

In addition to your full name, your contact page should include your business name if you have one, an e-mail address where they can contact you directly, and a phone number. If you don't have a business name, just use your name.

You don't have to post your phone number, but I highly recommend it because some people may be more comfortable calling you than e-mailing you. I've also gotten speaking engagements because people just pick up the phone. It was last minute and they didn't know how long it would take me to respond to their e-mail, so they just picked up the phone and said, "Hey, I want to talk to you about speaking at this event. It's in two weeks. Are you available?" Most of the time I've been able to say "Yes, I'm the last-minute speaker that you seek. Here are my fees. Here are my speaking topics."

You may want to have your business address on your site as well. It's not necessary, but an address does add to your credibility. People will trust you more if you post a physical address. Of course, that can be a PO Box. Going back to your Ready to Receive Checklist from Chapter Three, you don't have to have a fancy business address or an office. You may have a PO Box or use your home address.

People always ask about contact forms. You can have a contact form on your site, but I recommend that you still include your full contact information, because some people don't like using contact forms. Some people would rather e-mail or call you directly. This is all about making it easy for your potential client or customer. Make it easy for people to give you their money.

In naming your contact page, keep it simple. Use 'Contact,' 'Contact Me,' 'Connect with me' or 'Connect with *your name*.' Just keep it simple so that you don't confuse people.

Even if you don't have all three pages figured out yet, you can put up a 'Hire Me' page on your site and just let people know that you are for hire. When you meet people at networking events or you're just on the train telling people about your business, you can give them your site and they can at least get a feel for what you do.

That's really what we're getting at here: Make it easy for people to give you their money and to tell their friends about you or give you a referral. I'm going to give you the best tool to get referrals in Chapter Five, but having your website makes it easier for people to say, "Wow, have you heard of Happy Black Woman? This is her website." You can strengthen this effect with social proof.

Social Proof

Social proof just means that there's something or someone (besides you) who says you're worthy to do the work you do. You could talk about yourself all day long on your website, but when you have other third-party endorsements, that really helps. You can do this through social media, testimonials, or through any media or press that you've received. You'll want to add these things to your site so that people will be more likely to trust you.

There are many ways to show social proof, but here are a few of the main ones:

- **Social media statistics:** With social media, you can put widgets on your site that show the number of Twitter followers you have or the number of Facebook fans you have. You can put a Facebook 'Like' box on your site, which I highly recommend, so that people can connect with you.

  We'll talk more about social media in Chapter Five, but these are things that show people that you have followers online. It really doesn't matter how many you have, so don't be nervous about that if you only have 50 Twitter followers. As long as you have *some* followers, people will assume that you're some kind of leader in your industry and your business.

- **Subscribers:** If you have a newsletter and a blog, post how many subscribers you have on your site. When people sign up for my newsletter, I tell them that they've just joined a community of over 10,000 subscribers. That's a way to show social proof. Again, the numbers are really not that important. If you have 100 blog subscribers, that's pretty good. You just want people to know that they're not the first to discover you or think you're great.

- **Testimonials:** You can post testimonials on your site to show social proof. These can be testimonials from your former clients or customers. If you don't have any from paying clients yet, then use testimonials from people that you've helped for free. Giving you a testimonial is the least those people can do if you've been helping them with free coaching or consulting. As you get out there and people start asking you to give away your services, this is one way to make it a win/win situation. Offer something pro bono in exchange for a testimonial or a reference that you can post on your website.

If you give keynote speeches or workshops, post testimonials from attendees who were in the audience. These don't even have to be from people who paid to come, just attendees who say things like, "Wow, Julie's speech, The 20th Mile, was mind blowing. It really helped me sort out some things in my life." That is considered to be a testimonial.

If you provide services that people have used for free, go back and ask them, "Hey, remember that time I helped you plan your kid's birthday party? Would you be willing to write a couple of sentences about how good that was? I'm creating a website and

I need some testimonials from people." It's as simple as that. You don't have to make it difficult.

- **Press mentions or media appearances:** If you've been featured in the press, that's definitely a strong form of social proof. People view a press mention as an endorsement from a respected authority.

- **Honors and awards:** Any honors and awards you've received can also be posted as social proof. These should go in your bio on your 'About' page. If you have enough of them, you can create a separate page for awards and media. You may have received a lot of recognition for your work and experience, but you just haven't gotten paid for it yet. If so, let's capitalize on that and put it on your website so that it can help you attract paying clients.

- **Professional association memberships:** You can also show social proof using professional and association memberships. If you're a member of a professional organization that shows you're a professional, let people know that.

- **Existing or past clientele:** If you've worked with clients previously, even if they're not paying customers, post who you've worked with. If you did some work for a group pro bono or for a client for free, they were still your clients. They didn't pay you for your work, but no one has to know that. Posting who you've worked with can give you credibility. In fact, many potential clients will look at your client list before they look at your education or your credentials. If you've already worked with their peers, they will usually have more respect for you. If their peers thought you were good enough, you're probably good enough for them too. This is how social proof works.

- **Formal education credentials:** Of course, if you have a specific degree related to your business, definitely mention that on your site. Don't be concerned if you don't, as all of these other pieces can help you too.

Once you've gathered your different forms of social proof, where should you put them? One option is to create an additional page on your site. You could call it 'Testimonials.' On my site, I call it 'Success Stories.'

If you've only got one or two items and you don't need a whole page, another option is to post your testimonials on your 'About' page. The same goes for any press mentions or media appearances.

Even if you've only been on local TV or you had an interview on a blog, you can post that on your website as social proof. Your name was in lights at some point. Someone thought you were an expert enough to interview you or have you on his/her show or podcast. That can help people respect and trust you.

Conclusion

By now, you should be able to see how you can start making money with your business, even without having all of your ducks in a row yet. You don't have to have every single one of your services laid out from the beginning. You just need to define your signature product or service and get it out there.

I know I make it sound simple, and I know it's not. I want to recognize that, but I also want to encourage you. When you force yourself to put your information in these containers, you're light-years ahead of other people who are sitting back and saying, "I have all these ideas, but I don't know what to do with them!"

If you have ideas and you don't know what to do with them, that means you have all this potential income in your head—not in your bank account. I don't want you to sit on that potential income. I want that money to be in your life, contributing to your lifestyle and what you want to do with your life and your family. I want you to have all of those things that you identified in Chapter One as the reasons for starting your business.

If you haven't completed the homework for Chapter Three yet, I encourage you to do that. Completing it means that you're moving forward, doing the assignments, making progress, and getting closer to attracting more clients and customers. That's what this is all about.

Homework

1. If you don't have a website already, set up a free site on wordpress.com or get paid hosting.

2. Create your three main pages:

   a. 'About' Page

      i. Photo of you

      ii. Bio

         1. Your 'What I Do' statement

         2. Your expertise, credentials, and experience

         3. Why you started your business/your personal story

         4. What you do in your free time/possible connections

   a. 'Products and Services' Page: Use your Sales Page from Chapter Three here

   b. 'Contact' Page

      i. Your Full Name

  ii. Your Business Name

  iii. Email Address

  iv. Phone Number

  v. Physical Address

3. What social proof do you have? Add these things to your site, either as a new page or on your 'About' page.

  a. Social media

  b. Subscribers

  c. Testimonials

  d. Press mentions/Media appearances

  e. Honors and Awards

  f. Professional Association Memberships

  g. Existing or Past Clients

  h. Formal Education Credentials

4. Order business cards with your business information, including your website.

Setting up your website may have sounded daunting at the beginning of this chapter. I hope it appears more manageable now that I've broken it down into bite-sized pieces for you. At the very least, you can set up a free site on wordpress.com and set up your three pages. You now have guidelines on what to post on your pages, the language to use, and the information to include, so you can do it!

CHAPTER 5: GET OUT THERE

This chapter is about how to promote your business consistently and professionally. This is one of my favorite parts. I hope it will be yours, too, because I'm going to give you a ton of ideas on how to market your business without spending a lot of money.

In this chapter, you'll develop a low-cost marketing plan that you can use to build your business. You'll learn how to officially announce that you're open for business (You're really going to love the word-for-word e-mail template that I've given you that will take all the stress out of this part.). This book is called *Launch Your Business*, and that's what we're going to do.

Access the marketing plan template here: www.HappyBlackWoman. com/resources

One of the most important marketing strategies we'll cover is how to build your e-mail list, even if you're starting from scratch. I'm going give you some of my best strategies for getting your first leads. (Anyone who finds you through your e-mail list, your newsletter, or a blog post is considered to be a lead. Of course, they're people, too—you never want to look at them as just a number—but they're also potential clients or customers for your business.)

We're also going to go over the most effective use of social media. I'll give you some quick strategies to get started with blogging, Facebook, Twitter,

LinkedIn, YouTube, and Instagram. By no means do I recommend that you do all of those things, but you'll be able to pick one or two—maybe even three—to move forward with in your marketing plan.

We're going to help you attract new clients and customers on a small budget. Finally, we're going to put it all together and walk through how to create your marketing plan to start getting people interested in your business.

Tapping Your Existing Network

The people you already know can do a lot to help you in your business but, in order for that to happen, you have to let them know that you're open for business. It's important to do this in a direct, explicit way and keep updating them on a regular basis.

Why is this important? Because you are not the center of everyone's universe. Even if you've talked about your business to the people in your life (your friends, your family, your co-workers, your kids), they're not thinking about you that way. You have to officially announce that you're open for business so that people can see that you're serious and really understand what you're doing.

Although you may talk a lot about your business, when you're just starting out you may not talk about your business very confidently. For example, you might tell your friend, "I'm trying to get this speaking thing together." That doesn't really tell your friend anything. She doesn't know what kind of speeches you do, what types of audiences you want to speak for, what topics you speak on, what your speaking fees might be, how she can refer you, or what types of organizations you're looking to speak at. If she had that kind of information, she might be able to help you get more business. That's why you want to make sure that you alert people in a direct and explicit way. That's what the announcement e-mail is all about.

You want to start with your friends and family, making sure they understand what you do. You want to tap into this natural core group in your life because they can also connect you to new clients and customers. They want to share news about your business, but they can only do that if they clearly understand what you do.

You also want to alert your network of professional colleagues. If you're working a 9-to-5 job right now, there are probably some people within your network that you can call on and let them know what you're doing. Why would they be interested? Because people are nosy. They want to know what you've got going on. This is not the time to hide! Let people know what you're working on. It doesn't mean that you're going to quit your job or leave the industry. It just means that you have some exciting projects going on.

One way to do this is through LinkedIn. LinkedIn is a powerful networking community where you can contact your colleagues and tell them what you're up to.

You also want to set up phone calls and in-person meetings with people who might be interested in your business. Even now, you may have mentioned to some friends or colleagues that you're working on starting a business. If people are interested, they'll ask you to tell them more. For those people, if you haven't sent them any information yet, that's a missed opportunity. You want to set up phone calls and in-person meetings with people who seem interested in what you have to offer, and present it in a way that they can actually take action on.

For example, I recently had what I call a networking meeting. I met someone, and I was talking about the speaking topics that I have. It turned out that she had an upcoming conference, so it was a very clear opportunity to speak about potential business. We set up a time to meet at her office and talk further.

Be on the lookout for opportunities like this. Don't just send out the announcement e-mail and leave it at that. Follow up with the people who give you leads. For example, if someone says, "Your business sounds really cool. You should talk to Sally," make sure you get in touch with Sally. You never know what opportunities she might lead you to.

In this period of your business, you don't want to be passive. You're in launch mode, so everybody who has an interest is going to be someone that you want to follow up with and talk to. Your network is the place to start, because people who already know you will want to help you. This is where you can start getting some buzz.

I know this works, because I did it myself. I sent an announcement e-mail when I started my business, and I sent another one two years later when I was about to leave my job and take the business full-time. In the announcements, I basically said, "Hey, I'm embarking on this new business venture. Here's what it's about, and here's how you can help. Let me know if you're interested. Here's how you can stay in touch with me."

It was very effective. After I sent out that e-mail in the first month, people e-mailed me back and said things like, "Congratulations, that's great! I'll keep you in mind. If any of the organizations that I work with need a speaker, I'll refer you." And some people did. I started getting referrals for speaking engagements, and I'd ask how they found out about me. They'd say, "Oh, John forwarded me your information a few months ago." Thanks, John!

This is where networking comes in. If you let everyone in your life know what you're doing, then they can let other people know for you. Your announcement e-mail can be the start of your own little referral network.

In my workshops, some students have a lot of trepidation about this part. If you're thinking, "Oh my God, am I ready? Oh my God, if I send this out, everyone's going to know," you're not alone. But it's time to launch your business, and this is what launching is. It's announcing. It's telling everybody so that you can have your business officially open and ready to receive.

And here's a template that will make it easy for you to do this for yourself. You can also include an optional offer if you want to give a discount for new coaching clients, for instance. That could be an incentive for someone to take action and take you up on that offer.

Download the template at: www.HappyBlackWoman.com/resources

The thing is, before you send this e-mail, there are people in your world who don't even know what you're capable of doing and offering them, their organizations, or their families. They don't know whether you can offer coaching that's going to help them, or any services that can help them in their lives. They just know you in whatever role they already know you in. So now they will know you as a business owner. That's the most important thing here.

Part of your homework for this chapter is to write your announcement e-mail and send it. It won't do any good sitting on your computer—it has to go out! You can send it out via e-mail to all of your contacts in whatever e-mail service you use. You can send it to your LinkedIn network. You can send it to all of your work colleagues, all the people you know from church, all the people you know from your PTA group with your kids—anyone who knows you and might be interested in what you're doing. But the point is you've got to send it out. That makes your business real for the people in your network, and it makes it real for you, too.

Reaching People Who Don't Already Know You

Once you've announced your business to people who already know you, it's time to start connecting with people who don't know you. As you meet people and they express interest in what you're doing, you're going to want to have a way to follow up and make it easy for them to stay in touch with you. When you meet people at a networking event, you can give them your business card and take their cards, but it's very easy for them to forget about you if you don't keep them updated on your business. E-mail is one tool you can use to stay on people's minds and let them know about your new products and services.

E-mail List

To keep in touch with your leads, you'll need to create an e-mail list. You can use this to capture new leads for your business and to communicate with your existing prospects.

You may be wondering why I'm talking about e-mail and not social media. We'll cover social media too, but the fact is not everyone is on social media. Everyone checks their e-mail, though, and most people are in it all the time. That's why you want to use e-mail in addition to everything else that you're doing: people are more likely to see it and see it in time. Most people check their e-mail every day.

To set up an e-mail list, I recommend using either AWeber or MailChimp. Many beginning business owners choose MailChimp because it's free for up to 2,000 e-mail addresses on your e-mail list. As your business grows, your e-mail list will be one of your most valuable assets, so it's important to set it up with a good service from the start. AWeber and MailChimp are both good services for your e-mail list, and they give you clear instructions on how to get everything set up so you can start building your list.

The idea behind the e-mail list is that people can sign up on your website to receive your newsletters and blog posts. They can also receive information about your new products, promotions, sales, discounts, events—everything goes through e-mail. But how do you get people to sign up for it? One way is to give people a link to sign up for your newsletter in your announcement e-mail. Start by getting all the people you know onto your e-mail list and asking them to share the information with others.

The second way is to create a piece of valuable content that will benefit your ideal client or customer; I call this a free cupcake. You offer it to people who sign up for your e-mail list, and that's how you start a relationship with people and help them get to know you.

Offering Your Free Cupcake

What's your free cupcake? It's something people want. The reason why I call it a free cupcake is because nobody ever turns down a free cupcake. Think about it: Some people like cookies and some people don't, but everybody likes cupcakes. If you offer something free that everybody wants, then they will give you their name and e-mail address to get it. That's how you build your e-mail list.

For your free cupcake, you want to say something really valuable and put it in a free report, a guide, or a workbook that's related to your business. It could even be a free teleseminar or webinar. Many of my workshop participants find me by signing up for one of my free teleseminars or webinars, and then they become clients. That's how the process works. Once people sign up for your free cupcake, they're on your e-mail list and you can send them information. You can follow up and communicate with them. If they e-mail you questions, you can respond back to them, build that relationship, have one-on-one conversations, and offer them your products and services.

So this is how you can get your first 100 leads. I say 100 because every time I put out a free cupcake, it's very simple to get at least 100 people to sign up to get it. This was true even years ago when I created my first one. I think I had 120 people sign up for my first free cupcake.

Your first free cupcake doesn't have to be fancy. No one ever complains about a free cupcake. It was free, and it's a cupcake. What's there to complain about? So don't worry about whether yours is pretty enough or fancy enough. It's the content inside that's most important.

To help you think of what your free cupcake will be, here are some more examples of free content. Some of these are things I've created, and some were done by my students or clients. Either way, they're things that worked. This is not a random list of ideas for you; these are the things that work, so you can model your free content after one of these.

To give you one example, my current free cupcake is called *The Life Mapping Workbook: Design Your Ideal Life in Seven Key Areas.* I've had this free workbook on Happy Black Woman since 2011 or 2012, and I just keep updating it and making it better. It wasn't this pretty in the beginning; it was very basic. But the concept is the same.

The Life Mapping Workbook is a 14-page workbook. It helps you create your ideal life. That's my tagline—that's what I help people do.

In this workbook, I have you outline your ideal life in seven key areas. It's actually very simple. You can print it out and write in it, and it has changed people's lives. And people who have signed up for that and been added to my e-mail list are now more likely to sign up for my workshops. People often tell me in my workshops that this workbook is the first thing they got from me and, with it, they began to trust me and my information.

That's the power of your free cupcake. You want it to be really good—so good that you could be selling it, but you're giving it away for free. On the other hand, you don't want to put too much in it. I wouldn't want to give away a 40-page workbook; that's something that I really would be selling. A 14-page workbook is about the maximum that I would give away.

Another free cupcake that I've given away was a personal mission statement guide. This was my free cupcake when I had my first business as a nonprofit consulting and career coach. It was a four-page guide that took people through how to create a personal mission statement. That's something that's used in leadership development and personal development. When I gave that away on my website, I think I got 160 people to sign up for it in the first week that I launched. I put it all over Facebook and Twitter, and people were downloading it like crazy. So that was a really nice boost to my e-mail list because when people sign up for your freebie, they have to give you their names and e-mail addresses.

Here are a few other examples to give you an idea of the range of possibilities:

- One of my students in Launch Your Business Boot Camp created a Student Debt Planner. It's a two-page Excel tool that she created, where you can type in how much money you owe on your student loans and it tells you how much money you need to have available depending on how many years you want to pay it down. It's a great tool, and when she created it and put it in the Facebook group for the class, people went crazy about it. She got a lot of people on her e-mail list from our class that way. That's when you know it's a good free cupcake, because she could really charge for that. It's a two-page tool, but it could save people a lot of time and energy. And she offered a coaching program that helps students pay off their student loans faster than usual, so it leads right into her service.

- One of my clients did a 60-minute free webinar. She has a great YouTube following, but she was trying to build her e-mail list. Her webinar was called Seven Steps to Go Vegan with Your Family, and she offers vegan coaching and training. That was her cupcake, and she got a ton of people to sign up.

- Another free cupcake that I've used is a teleseminar that I gave away on my nonprofit website a few years ago. It was called Six Ways to Rock Your Nonprofit Career. For those of you who want to make money with speaking, take note: This was also the title of one of my signature speech topics. So, if an organization wanted to hear me speak, they could just download this free 60-minute audio. Not only did it allow them to hear me and make them want to hire me, but it also gave me their e-mail address. From then on they'd keep getting my weekly articles, my blog posts, and information about my products and services, so that they couldn't forget about me unless they unsubscribed. That's the thing: You want to be top-of-mind, because people have a lot of things going on.

- I've also created a Young Nonprofit Professional's Career Guide. This was a 12-page resource directory. It's one of the first information products I put together, and I didn't even really create any content for it. I just made a listing of all the different resources that young nonprofit professionals could use. I didn't have to create anything—I just went online and looked up the places where they can go and get books, low-cost training for their careers, and other resources. But it was valuable to people because I had gathered all of this information into one place to make it easy for them. Even if you don't have any content that you feel you can put into a free cupcake yet, you can always make a resource directory.

- Another free cupcake that many coaches and consultants offer is a 30-minute strategy session. You may be wondering whether 30 minutes is too long to do a free session. My answer is no! When you're selling somebody a package that may be $1,000 or more, he or she is going to want to talk to you first. People usually don't just buy something off the internet when it's at that price point, so it's definitely worth the time to talk to somebody for 30 minutes if the return is going to be that high. Even if they don't buy that day, guess what? When they're ready to buy, they're going to come to you, because most people haven't taken the time to actually talk to them for 30 minutes.

There's actually a psychological basis for offering a free cupcake and why it works. It's called the law of reciprocity, and it comes from Robert Cialdini's book, *Influence*. The law of reciprocity says that when you give someone something for free, that person wants to help you in return. Psychologically, they feel that they should give you something back. So if you give someone something free, whether it's a workbook or a webinar or a 30-minute free session over the phone, they have in their minds that they need to pay you back. They can do that by purchasing something from you that they already know they need, or by telling their friends about you.

I have many people in my community who have never purchased anything from me, but they send their friends to my events, and they tell their friends they should buy my products. I ask people how they found out about me, and they often say, "Oh, my friend so-and-so. She reads your blog all the time." Mind you, I don't know her friend's name because her friend never buys anything from me, but she helps me out by sending her friends to me.

That's the power of your free cupcake. It's actually one of the most powerful tools you can use in your business. In addition to posting it on your website, you can also print it and give it out when you do speaking engagements, or send it to people when you're networking and you want to send them a little taste of what you do in your business. That can be very, very powerful.

Blogging

Once you have your e-mail list and your free cupcake set up, my next recommendation is to start blogging. You may be wondering what you'll send out to your e-mail list every week. One thing you'll send out is your blog articles.

If you don't have a blog, you want to set one up. We talked about this in Chapter Four—you can put up a free site or host one with Bluehost.

When I talk about blogging, the big question I always get is: How often should I post to my blog? It's very important that you post something at least once a week. I actually post more often than that because the more you post on your blog, the more traffic you get. People always want to know what's new. If you haven't written anything new in weeks, people tend to forget about you. The internet is a very big place, so you want to remain top-of-mind.

The same goes for your newsletter. At the very least, you should send out your blog articles to your mailing list once a week. Don't skip a week, or people will forget you. If you want people to buy something from you, you have to get them used to hearing from you regularly.

For your blog, there are two types of blog posts that you can use to earn money. One is direct promotional posts, and the other is indirect promotional posts. With a direct promotional post, you announce a new product or service. For example, I may post on the Happy Black Woman blog about an upcoming class on finding your purpose. I'll tell a story in the post to get people interested and paying attention, but at the end it's very clear: We're having a class. Here's what the class is about. Here's where you can learn more and buy the class.

Many new business owners seem hesitant to do that, but it's something you have to do. Don't try to be all clever and cute and think people are going to figure out that you have something to sell. Don't make your potential client or customer work too hard to figure out what you're offering. Your blog can be a great place to just be very blatant about it: I'm selling a product; let me tell you all about it.

You can also do indirect promotional posts, where you can talk about how to do something and then say, "Hire me if you want me to help you do it one-on-one." For instance, one of my students makes favors for wine glasses so you can tell whose is whose. She could do a post about how to plan a themed party for your graduating senior. Once she's talked about how to plan that party, she can add that if you're having wine or champagne, you might want to have some of my custom wine glass favors to really make your theme pop.

This is more of an indirect way to promote your business. Remember, blogging won't work for your business if you don't promote your business on your blog. If you look on my blog (http://happyblackwoman.com/blog), you can see an example of the types of blog posts that I've put out there. If you look around, you'll see that some of them are very blatantly promotional. But people still read them because people are nosy. And guess what? Some of those nosy people end up buying stuff. That's not business-speak, but it's true: nosy people buy stuff.

Facebook

Next we'll talk about Facebook. You want to use Facebook to promote your business. Why? Because everyone's on Facebook. With that many people, you know that some of them will be interested in what you have to offer.

For your business, it's important to create a page, not a personal profile. Use your headshot as a profile photo on your Facebook page, and make sure you mix up the content. You want to have photos, videos, quotes, blog posts, and updates—not just one type of content.

The key is to post on Facebook at least once a day. You don't want to let that page go for a long time, because you don't want to give people reason to wonder if you're serious about this.

You also want to post about your products and services at least once a day. If you're only posting once a day, then obviously you want to post about your products and services less than that, but you can offer fan-only sales and discounts. For example, you could offer 50% off for all of your Facebook fans. Give people a reason to buy.

To give you an example, you can check out my Facebook page here:

https://www.facebook.com/happyblackwoman

Keeping your Facebook page very active can yield you great results, but it does take some time. If you're going to do social media, I recommend that you pick one or two of these platforms and go all the way with them. Don't try to do all of them if you're not going to do any of them well. Really, the top two I recommend are blogging and Facebook. All of the other ones are extra. I can't tell you how many people have found my business through Facebook. I'm not that fond of Facebook overall and I don't use it in my personal life, but it's been very profitable for my business.

If you have something that you're promoting, Facebook is a great place to put it. It would be very silly of me not to use Facebook to promote my upcoming events. My Facebook page has over 110,000 fans now, and people ask me, "How did you get that many fans in such a short time?" I used Facebook ads for $5.00 a day. For about six months, my Facebook marketing budget was about $150 a month. I think I spent about $1,000 on that in total, and it got me so many fans that I've made that back many times over. It's a very good investment if you want to build your page up to a large number.

Again, the whole point of this is to get people interested in your business. I don't care about likes for likes' sake. I care about people who like the page and start interacting with me, and all of a sudden they're at my event in Atlanta and they have an experience of learning and networking that changes their lives. That's what I care about.

You may find social media frustrating, and I get it, but it's not really about social media. It's about growing your business. If I could do what I do without Facebook, I would. But it's been very beneficial, so I stick with it.

Twitter

Another great channel that you can use to promote your business is Twitter. If you don't have an account yet, you'll want to get one set up and put the Twitter icon on your website.

The way you get traction from Twitter is by sharing the links to your blog posts. When you publish something, use Twitter to let people know you have a new post.

If you use Twitter, you should Tweet at least once a day about your business. I see people with Twitter accounts and they don't even have their business website in their profile—no mention that they even have a business. Why be on Twitter if you're not going to use it to promote your business? If you're on Twitter and you're just yapping, shooting the breeze, and making jokes about celebrities, you're doing it wrong. First of all, you're wasting your time, and secondly, you're not making money.

Instead, I tell people when I have a new blog post. When people see that, they read it, and many of them will also share it. I also use Twitter to promote my products and services. For example, if I were offering a new session of the Launch Your Business Boot Camp, I would send out tweets to promote it. To see what my Twitter account looks like, you can check it out here:

https://twitter.com/happyblackwoman

You don't have to be generic with your social media. You can be as detailed as you want. You also don't need separate business and personal accounts. I recommend that you just have one account. Otherwise it gets too confusing.

YouTube

Another tool that you can use to promote your business is YouTube. If you don't have a YouTube account, you can create one. And again, put the icon on your site.

One great way to use YouTube is to make how-to videos or tutorials related to your product or service. I like to make videos announcing things, too. Whatever you have going on, you should use the tools available to you, and this one is free. I make a video on my computer, I put it up on YouTube, and people are looking at it. It might be the tipping point for someone making a decision to join me for an event.

I call this your low-cost marketing plan because you don't need to do anything that's expensive. You really don't. All you have to do is be consistent and courageous. You don't have to put yourself in front of the camera, but it can help. You can also request video testimonials from your clients. I have two great video testimonials on YouTube from students in my Blogging School course. It really helps people to see those—it builds trust.

For my YouTube channel, I don't really get fancy; I just do the bare minimum. You can see my channel here: https://www.youtube.com/user/happyblackwoman_

I'm not trying to get famous on YouTube—that's not the goal. The goal is to build my business. If somebody finds me on YouTube and then goes to my website and signs up for my e-mail list, that's what I want. I'm not trying to be popular. A lot of people think they need to increase their YouTube subscribers, but you don't. You need to increase your *e-mail* subscribers. You can send your e-mail subscribers information about your products and services; you can't send messages like that on YouTube. You can only make another video, and not everybody will watch it. But if you can e-mail them, more people will read that e-mail.

You have to be smart and strategic about this, and the longer you stay in the Happy Black Woman community, the more these concepts will be burned into your brain. You're not trying to be popular; you're trying to be profitable.

Instagram

Instagram is another social media channel. It's relatively new, and it's owned by Facebook now. Instagram can be very good at helping you spread the word about your business through photographs. So if you don't have an Instagram account, you want to get one. Again, put the icon on your website.

To use Instagram, you just show a photo of your product or service. For someone who has a physical product, it would be great to show pictures of the product and how it's used. For example, my client who makes wine glass charms could show the charms on different types of wine glasses or at different parties. But you don't need to have a physical product to use Instagram. Even if you have a service, you can show photos of the lifestyle that you're promoting.

For example, I have a client who is a health coach. She posts photos of herself in healthy environments. She'll post pictures of what she eats for a healthy breakfast or where she goes to walk in the morning to meditate and pray, and people love it. They love knowing what's in her smoothie. They love knowing how many miles she walked that day. If you're that kind of coach, people really start to respect you because they feel that you practice what you preach.

On my Instagram, I give a behind-the-curtains glimpse of my personal life so people can see that Happy Black Woman really is all about living a life of happiness, success, and freedom. I talk about my business success, I talk about my happiness, I talk about living in Hawaii, and I talk about freedom. I also post inspirational quotes. That shows people that I really live the things I talk about.

When you create an Instagram profile, make sure you put the link to your website in your profile. You can see mine as an example here: http://instagram.com/happyblackwoman.

LinkedIn

LinkedIn can also be very effective in promoting your business if you use it consistently. For your LinkedIn account, set up your profile, add your bio, and add a link to your site. Clearly identify your business in your headline. Also, include your headshot. This should be you, not a picture of your dog or your child. This is to represent your business, so you want it to be professional.

Once you have your profile set up, use it to keep in touch. Send your announcement e-mail to the people in your LinkedIn network.

For example, you can see my LinkedIn profile here: http://www.linkedin.com/in/rosettathurman

You can see that my headline states very clearly: "Founder and CEO of HappyBlackWoman.com." What I do is professional training and coaching. Where I live: Honolulu, Hawaii. It's very clear, and then I have my bio in the summary box.

When it comes to social media, just as with your free cupcake, you want to focus on your ideal client. Who is she and what does she want? What does she struggle with? Why does she need me? Where does she hang out?

You're not trying to offer people what you want to give them; you're offering them what they want. You're offering them solutions to their problems. Don't give people a book of poems because you want to write a book of poems and give it out to people for free. That's probably not what they want. You really want to focus on your ideal client and what she wants and needs, and find a way to give her that.

Networking

In all this talk of social media, don't forget the original way to be social: in person. When it comes to networking, you want to make sure you have your business cards ready and have at least one networking event on your calendar per week. You may even want to do more than that. If you're in a city with a lot of professionals, business owners, and other people in your ideal client market, you might have lots of networking events throughout the month. This is a great chance to meet new people and grow the reach of your business.

Low-Cost Marketing Plan

As you think about all of this and put it together, you may start to feel like it's too much. It's OK if you don't get to everything on your plan. It's better to say, "I'm going to do four networking events," even if you only end up doing two.

So, as you write your Low-Cost Marketing Plan, here's what you'll want to include:

- **Blog**. You want to write and post one article a week.

- **E-mail newsletter.** You want to send this out weekly. Set up your account with AWeber or MailChimp. Then, when you post your blog, make sure you put the same article into your newsletter.

- **Social media.** Which one, two, or three social media platforms are you going to focus on? Choose up to three and just do those really well.

- **Networking.** Plan at least one event per week to attend and meet people in person.

- **Business cards**. If you don't have any yet, the person who did my blog header for Happy Black Woman is Carina Kellogg, and she does phenomenal work. If you need someone to design your business cards for you, reach out to her and tell her that Happy Black Woman sent you. She did really great work for me.

Homework

1. Write and send your announcement e-mail. If you've already sent something like this in the past, it could be an update e-mail, like "Hi everybody. I'm updating you on my business. I'm building it, I'm growing it, and I'm excited about it." Even if you think you've already done this, don't skip this assignment. After all the work you've done throughout this book, you'll be much clearer on your business. It's time to make sure your family and friends are, too.

2. Figure out what your free cupcake is going to be. I gave you a lot of great ideas; now it's time to choose what you're going to offer. If you already have a free cupcake, you might think about how you can improve what you have.

3. Develop your low-cost marketing plan. Out of all the things that we talked about in this chapter, I want you to write out your action steps for your marketing plan. What will you do for:

   a. Your blog

   b. Your e-mail newsletter

   c. Your free cupcake

   d. Social media

   e. Networking

   f. Business cards

Include exactly what steps you'll take and dates you'll have them accomplished by. If you commit to when you'll do these things, they'll get done much faster.

READY TO LAUNCH YOUR BUSINESS?

Here's Your Next Step...

Now that you have my proven 5-step solution to getting paid to do what you love, it's time to take action! This is my invitation to help you take the next step to finally get your dream business off the ground.

Introducing...

The Launch Your Business Virtual Boot Camp! You can learn more about the course at LaunchYourBusinessBootCamp.com.

This 6-week online training will show you EXACTLY how to build a profitable business doing what you love so that you can quit your job and finally have the freedom to travel and live life on YOUR terms!

In my own journey, what I know for sure is that if hadn't taken that first leap of faith, I know I wouldn't have the business, lifestyle or freedom I have today.

At some point, you have to take the leap.

You have to start NOW, no matter how scary it seems.

It's the only way you will ever get to where you want to be.

What if, instead of just wishing that things were different, you gave your dedicated focus to your business for 6 full weeks?

I'm sure you would begin to see big results and new possibilities, just like I've been able to do in my own business.

Instead of waiting for SOMEDAY, you might be surprised at what's truly possible for you to do TODAY.

I talk to women all over the world that have wonderful ideas, but unfortunately just have some significant gaps in their strategy and implementation.

You may need support in your business right now if:

- You don't have a consistent weekly schedule. You only work on your business when you "feel like it" or when you get "inspired." As a result, your productivity is inconsistent, as well as your income.

- You don't have clarity about what you do and who you serve. You stumble when someone asks you to describe your business. And you're not quite sure who your ideal client is or where to find them.

- You don't have a viable business model. You don't have a viable business model. You have a good business idea for how you want to help people, but there's no income generation plan in place to ensure you get clients and customers each month.

- You don't have accountability. There's no one in your life to hold you accountable to your business goals and make sure you get things done each and every week – no excuses. You don't have a marketing plan.

- You still haven't finished your website, you're not blogging at least once a week, social media is an afterthought. You go to networking events every once in a while and you never have business cards to pass out.

- You're not charging enough money for your products and services. You don't feel confident in yourself and what you have to offer yet, so you give away your stuff for free or at a price so low that you're actually LOSING money with every sale.

So now I have to ask you...

Is it time for you to take action and finally start making some real money in your business this year?

When you register for the course at LaunchYourBusinessBootCamp. com, you will master my five-step solution to get paid to do what you love so that you can quit your job and have the freedom to travel and live life on your own terms.

Step 1: Get Focused - How to Transform Your Mindset and Make Time for Your Business

When you're just starting out, it can be challenging to figure out how to stay focused and manage your time. This session will teach you exactly how to stop treating your business like a hobby and get serious about making real money doing what you love!

Step 2: Get Clarity - How to Find Your Sweet Spot and Identify Your Ideal Client

It's difficult to move forward in your business when you still don't know what your business actually is! This session will help you get crystal clear on your "sweet spot" and hone in on the people you are best positioned to serve with your products and services.

Step 3: Get Paid - How to Create Products and Services That People Are Willing to Pay For

You can't make money in your business without having products and services available that people can buy. This session will show you exactly how to get paid by creating the right programs, packages and pricing that will have your ideal clients and customers ready to purchase from you!

Step 4: Get Online - How to Create or Improve Your Website

Are you tired of being embarrassed when people ask for the link to your website because it's still "under construction" and has been for way too long? These days, people expect every business (no matter how small!) to have an online presence where they can learn more about you and your company. This session will show you how!

Step 5: Get Out There - How to Promote Your Business Professionally and Consistently

If you want to build a successful business, you have to let people know who you are and what you have to offer. This session will teach you simple, low-cost ways to market your business and bring in consistent clients, customers and sales.

When you register now, you will also receive these valuable bonuses!

BONUS #1: A Ticket to Rosetta's Next Launch Your Business LIVE 3-Day Boot Camp!

This will be a 3-day high-level training and networking event where you can experience the loving spirit of the women in our Happy Black Woman Community and be fully supported in building your business! When you attend Rosetta's Launch Your Business LIVE 3-Day Boot Camp, you will get the chance to learn from her directly and be in community with dozens of like-minded entrepreneurs. Rosetta will walk you, step by step, through each of the 5 training modules in person so that you can implement what you've learned and ask questions right there at the event! This interactive training focuses on giving you a deeper understanding of her 5-step system that shows you exactly how to launch, relaunch and grow your business this year.

BONUS #2: Access to the LIVE 2016 Launch Your Business Virtual Boot Camp!

Now, you get to take the complete self-paced Launch Your Business Virtual Boot Camp program AND still receive access to the next LIVE run of the course with 6 weeks of training and Q&A with Rosetta and our cohort of women entrepreneurs for 2016. PLUS: Each year, Rosetta UPDATES the course with additional content, strategies and tools to help you build your business!

So again, my question to you is:

Are you ready to launch your business?

To get started, visit the link below and get enrolled today:

LaunchYourBusinessBootCamp.com

ABOUT THE AUTHOR

Rosetta is the founder of HappyBlackWoman.com, a supportive community that empowers women all over the world to create lives of happiness, success and freedom through personal development and entrepreneurship.

As a transformational coach and mentor, Rosetta teaches women how to create profitable online businesses doing what they love so that they can quit their jobs and finally have the freedom to travel and live life on their own terms. Her clients and students value her "tough love" approach to helping them reach their big goals faster than they ever thought possible.

Rosetta holds a Master's Degree in Organizational Management and has also taught leadership, business and marketing courses as an Adjunct Professor at Trinity Washington University.

Rosetta is an avid traveler and her favorite city is Honolulu, Hawaii. She strives to live a simple, minimalist lifestyle – everything she owns fits into one suitcase! When she's not writing or teaching, Rosetta enjoys good food, good music and good bourbon. Preferably all at the same time!

73702567R00068

Made in the USA
Columbia, SC
15 July 2017